# THE HOMESCHOOL
# ALTERNATIVE

Incorporating a Homeschool Mindset for
the Benefit of Black Children in America

DR. MYIESHA TAYLOR & HALEY TAYLOR SCHLITZ

"*We need to stop believing the myth. In this country, what we call education is actually indoctrination. And it takes us from the age of 5 to the age of 18 to thoroughly indoctrinate people so they will believe in the myth of white superiority.*"

– Jane Elliott

# Note about this book

While this manuscript is a criticism of public school, it is not a suggestion that they shouldn't exist. The idea of public school is a noble one—where a country taxes itself to invest in the next generation. In homogeneous countries where every child looks like everybody's child, it is much easier to elicit mass support for society's children. However, in our heterogeneous American society, often Black and brown students don't look like everybody's child, so building a beneficial system for them is fraught with obstacles and ulterior motives.

Outlining the history of America while including relevant facts about embedded racism is truth-telling. It is important to talk about issues that affect marginalized groups, even if it's uncomfortable to hear. It is only through open discussion and dedicated action that race equity in America can ever be achieved.

This is a book that reminds us of the history upon which America evolved into the country we are experiencing today, particularly with regard to education. This is a book that advocates for parents to empower themselves and rebuke the brainwashing of the media and our own schooling to envision alternative points of view—particularly the option of homeschooling.

This is a book that gives parents who find that public school is their best option overall strategies and techniques that will help them realize that even in utilizing public, or private, schools, they have options for enrichment and 'homeschooling' that will enhance their child's journey to adulthood.

Caveat stated up front: While the argument is made that homeschooling is the most tailored method of educating a child—and the book was written to advocate for this option—nowhere is it mentioned that other methods cannot work. No one method works for all children and families. And a method that worked for a period of time, may not work the next time. It needs to be emphasized that what's best for a child is multifaceted and includes sane parents, a working household, a certain amount of income, and good family dynamics. Realizing the reality that homeschooling may not be best for a family (even if it's best for an individual child from an academic perspective) is of paramount importance. It is counterproductive to homeschool if the family were to end up on the street. Just like paying for a fancy private school may be great for the individual child's education, if it bankrupts the family, the overall benefit is negated and shouldn't be done.

It is up to all of us to make individual and independent decisions for ourselves and for our children while considering a myriad of factors. Those reading this book are assumed to be already exploring alternatives to traditional public school, and we attempt to walk you through the mental gymnastics that many Black American homeschoolers struggle with.

# A Mother's Intuition

## By Dr. Myiesha Taylor

More than anything else in life, I've always wanted a little girl. My own "real-life" baby doll. Unbothered by the opinions of others, I played with dolls long after it was socially acceptable and even took my two favorite dolls with me to college. Every important decision I've made in my life was informed by an inner spirit that rejected arbitrary expectations, from the college that I selected to the sorority I joined. Novelty is disruptive and is the impetus of forward progress.

When I had my daughter, I knew my most important life's purpose had arrived. The legacy of my family has been one of self-realization through lifelong education, and I was eager to get this new baby girl on board. Due to a variety of reasons, our search for the right educational environment took us through five preschools before kindergarten. In a combination of private, public, and religious schools, we pieced together a great academic program that met our needs year to year.

During school breaks, I implemented what I called "Taylored Curriculum." Taylored Curriculum was a set of lessons and experiences that supplemented and enriched the standard academic education that my children received at traditional school. It was a time to introduce spirituality, culture, politics, self-love, as well as encourage self-expression and appreciation of life. It was a time to "undo" all the madness that traditional school injects into the lives of children. Taylored Curriculum allowed me to be the involved and informed mother that I longed to be and reconnect to the entire reason I wanted this real-life baby doll.

Then fifth grade happened. And there wasn't enough time to undo all the stuff that school was doing to my child. Coupled with the gaps in knowledge and the overemphasis on standardized exams, I felt in my heart that something had to change. And after being in seven schools in 10 years, I was wise enough to know that more of the same schools were not going to yield different results.

While I'm a disruptor and actually feel most alive when I'm marching to the beat of my own drum, my husband is more comfortable in established, safe spaces. As such, I had to convince him to let me pull our daughter out of the only type of school system we knew and put the burden of educating her square on our shoulders. Apprehensive at first but feeling my passion and dedication to this project, he conceded, and we agreed to regular reevaluations.

To our own amazement, we watched our child regain her confidence, spunk, leadership tendencies, and wonder. She transformed from reluctant math student to a self-professed "Mathelete"—going on to excel in national math competitions and accelerating from fifth grade math to pre-calculus in three short years! Gone was the "mean girl drama" that consumed many in her peer group. We no longer had to gracefully educate well-meaning white teachers and school administrators on how the choice in music at assemblies or roles assigned in school performances were racist and completely inappropriate. All of our energy could be focused on doing rather than un-doing.

I am often asked, "How did you know to pull your child out of school? Did something happen?"

The answer is I don't know if I consciously had the capacity to completely think it through, anticipate results, or really know what to do.

My only guide was a voice from within and a feeling of uneasiness. It didn't feel right to drop my child off at some governmental institutional building for 40 hours a week and then have to ask permission of these strangers to see her and take her out to spend a day with me. It didn't feel right to have parent-teacher conferences in which an annual new stranger was trying to tell me all about my child's "problems." As they identified ways she didn't "fit in" or follow rules, they failed to celebrate her independent spirit and her inquisitive mind. They were not privy to the behind-the-scenes (anti)social shenanigans that are rampant in "mean girl circles" and how that may affect in-class group projects. In short, they didn't know her, or her situation, like I knew her. And it didn't feel right for me to delegate the huge honor and responsibly of shaping her heart and mind, creating the very way she sees herself in the world, to random people who don't really know her. That was a travesty and very irresponsible.

My mother intuition knew better. And when you know better, you do better.

# Lioness

## By Haley Taylor Schlitz

When I was in third grade, I remember being in class with one of my favorite teachers. We read a book about four different animals going on a journey together, and then in class, we assigned each animal to various classmates based on the characteristics of the animal and the classmate. I recall the description of a golden retriever. A golden retriever was fun, kind, gentle, friendly, and pretty. Everybody loved the golden retriever. I wanted to be the golden retriever. I proclaimed to the class that I would be the golden retriever, to which various classmates immediately refuted, "YOU?! You are no golden retriever! You are more like a lion. Or a seal." The seal was the class clown—always super funny and goofy but was always causing trouble because of his/her silliness. The lion, though, was the protecting and wise leader, more known for his/her mean personality traits. The lion was the one who was rude and never laughed at a joke, always serious. The lion was not gentle and scared away all the little butterflies, unlike the golden retriever who was gentle enough to interact with the butterflies without scaring them off.

My feelings were so hurt. No one would ever like the lion. The lion had no friends. I set out to prove to these schoolmates that I was more like the golden retriever than the lion. Instead of suggesting games to play, I sat quietly and smiled. When someone disrespected me or others, I didn't speak up. In order to fit in, I tried to mimic behaviors and attitudes.

One day in fifth grade, I shared with my mom that one of my

friends decided to ditch school and go to the local Burger King. She tried to get me to jump through a hole in the fence, but I didn't like Burger King. My mom asked me if I told anyone at school, like a teacher. I told her I hadn't because that would undermine the golden retriever persona I was trying to master.

I remember friendships at school being superficial and distracting. I remember sitting in class bored, as the teacher droned on about some topic that either I found utterly irrelevant, completely disempowering to me as a Black person, or totally uninteresting as I already knew the information. Imagine being forced to sit through a bad movie where all the people that look like you are the villains, where you are bored because you've seen this movie multiple times and cannot fast-forward through particularly boring parts or commercials. That is what traditional school was like for me. But instead of it only being a two-hour movie, it was a prospect of eight years—just to get out of high school! Then there was college, graduate school, and possibly more.

When my mom finally suggested homeschooling, I had no idea what that would mean. But I knew I'd get to choose more of what I did with my time. I knew that I wouldn't have to prove myself worthy of existing to my educators. I knew I could be myself without judgment. I knew that I would be spending time with my favorite people. I had no reason to doubt the wisdom of the mother I'd been blessed to be born to. And I was very grateful that my innate value was appreciated, and my inner lioness was nurtured.

# Why Consider Homeschooling?

Compulsory public education in the United States of America was established in the late 1800s and early 1900s as a reaction to the public's fear of a changing America. Hate groups such as the Ku Klux Klan were afraid that immigrants were not "Americanizing" and were concerned that private parochial schools, particularly Catholic schools, were becoming too influential. Movements were made to implement public schooling and integrate the schools, so all students learned "their places" in society.

The history and evolution of traditional schooling and formal education administration in America is haphazard and arbitrary. Traditional schools are a product created to fulfill a societal need and have nothing to do with ensuring that children pursue educational paths that lead to innovation and independent thinking. On the contrary, with the industrial revolution and the necessity to produce workers that could function in factories, school became the training mechanism to produce good workers.

Traditional schools group students by birth year and proximity to a building. In aliquots of 20, they form a class where each individual child, regardless of his/her biology, interests, emotional state, or history, is expected to move lock-step along his/her personal educational journey with the random students that happen to be in the same cohort. Additionally, a new stranger—we call them a classroom teacher—is charged with getting to know each child and shepherding him/her through a state-mandated set of material. Come spring, the child is tested on his/her acquisition of said material, and if he/she cannot regurgitate enough of it on demand, he/she is considered a failure.

When we discuss homeschooling, particularly with parents of color, there is a resistance because for many years we fought for the right to integrate and attend the "good" schools—which happened to require a bus and inter-district transfer to the white schools. All of this progress, and the right to sit shoulder-to-shoulder with the majority, must mean we've won. To suggest that we should go back to educating our children ourselves is a huge step backwards, the rationale implores.

However, the school system was never designed for students to become independent, critically thinking, problem-solving leaders. And when the added race component is considered, where multiple studies have demonstrated that Black students are disproportionally disciplined and disrespected in public schools, it is any wonder why any parent of a child of color would subject their son or daughter to such a system.

# Book Outline

## Part 1: The Why? Setting the Stage

Part One is a short trip that considers what life is like moving through the world in brown bodies as Americans—from becoming American to being Black, and finally as school children.

## Part 2: The What? Homeschooling as an Educational Option

Part Two explores homeschooling—what it means, the correct mindset, how to get started, and then how to be successful.

**Part 3: The How? A Guide to Homeschooling
and Frequently Asked Questions**

# Part 1: The Why?

## Setting the Stage

# Chapter 1: Historical Perspective
## Being A Black American

### Colonization and Slavery

*"Perhaps the easiest way to understand why colonialism was so horrific is to imagine it happening in your own country now. It is invaded, conquered, and occupied by a foreign power. Existing governing institutions are dismantled and replaced by absolute rule of the colonizers. A strict hierarchy separates the colonized and the colonizer; you are treated as an inconvenient subhuman who can be abused at will. The colonists commit crimes with impunity against your people. Efforts at resistance are met with brutal reprisal, sometimes massacre."* – Nathan J. Robinson (A Quick Reminder of Why Colonialism Was Bad, *Current Affairs*)

Modern humans, Homo sapiens, developed in the Horn of Africa about 200,000 years ago. About 150,000 years ago, modern humans migrated out of east Africa to gradually populate the world. There were some natural barriers that delayed human migration to faraway lands. Indigenous genetic studies suggest that North and South America are the last continents to have gained human inhabitation about 20,000 years ago (so about 18,500 years before Columbus was even born).

In this pre-Columbian era, civilizations thrived. There is

archaeologic evidence of very sophisticated civilizations on the continent, including urban centers, written languages, record archiving, monuments, government, and hierarchies. In the 1400s, European colonization began. Upon European colonists' arrival, many cities were destroyed, libraries burned, and re-education was done to convert native non-Christians to Christianity. Further, it is estimated that between 80 and 90% of the Native American populations diminished after European arrival due to disease and conflicts, mass murders of natives by colonists, and enslavement.

As American society transitioned to agriculture-based culture, coupled with the colonizers trade agreements, it became necessary to import labor. Africa already had a history of slavery and providing slaves for the Europeans was akin to exporting any other good. Africans were not deemed inferior initially; however, in an America where poor whites were being manipulated by the elite and facing the same struggle of servitude with the same limited options as Africans, the concept of "whiteness" was introduced to placate their suffering by suggesting that they were at least better off than the African slave.

## Being Traumatized

*"Researchers have long investigated how historical trauma is passed down through the generations, and findings suggest actual memories are transmitted through the DNA for Jews, Native Americans, and other groups, DeGruy indicates. That same concept can be applied to the impact of slavery on African-Americans."*

*"PTSS differs from post-traumatic stress disorder (PTSD), which results from a single trauma*

*experienced directly or indirectly.* 'When we look at
American chattel slavery, we are not talking about a
single trauma; we're talking about multiple traumas
over lifetimes and over generations,' says DeGruy.
'Living in Black skin is a whole other level of stress.'"
– Cindy George (Do You Have Post-Traumatic Slave
Syndrome? *Ebony*)

There is a fascinating concept called genetic memory. Genetic
memory is the concept that extremely traumatic events in a
human's life affects and/or alters their DNA. In so doing, their
progeny then shares the trauma of their ancestors. Research has
demonstrated this in some of the most basic forms via laboratory
rodents. In these experiments, lab rats are put into a maze. Once
they learn the maze, it has been observed that their offspring
seem to navigate the maze without as much effort.

Additionally, studies on mice have demonstrated that trans-
generational inheritance of behavior is evidenced in mice and olfactory stimuli. When mice were conditioned to behave in a certain way to olfactory stimuli prior to conception, their offspring
for two generations demonstrated that same conditioned behavior
despite not having been conditioned themselves.

It is suggested that many of our natural human instincts are
more aptly described as genetic memories whereby ancestors
learned by process of elimination how to survive, and that information is passed down to their children and grandchildren such
that their survival will be enhanced.

However, when these genetic memories are the result of tre-
mendous and horrific trauma, the lasting effects on subsequent
generations are likewise present. Studies show that there is evidence in Holocaust survivors that the trauma they suffered is

capable of being passed on to their children; specifically in how their offspring are able to deal with stress.

## The Trauma of Slavery

A full account of the atrocities of slavery are beyond the scope of this book. Suffice it to say, the Transatlantic Slave Trade was one of the most horrific migrations in human history. The journey was months long where humans were chained together in sweltering, foul, and unsanitary conditions below deck in cargo packing. Women and children were often kept on deck so the crew could repeatedly rape and torture them. Disease was common, and it was normal and expected for a death rate to reach 40%.

One firsthand account was documented by Olaudah Equiano. He was originally from the Ibo people along the Niger River in Africa. He was captured, endured the Middle Passage, and later acquired his freedom becoming a popular abolitionist. He wrote in his autobiography in 1789:

> *"The closeness of the place, and the heat of the climate, added to the number in the ship, which was so crowded that each had scarcely room to turn himself, almost suffocated us. This produced copious perspirations, so that the air soon became unfit for respiration, from a variety of loathsome smells, and brought on a sickness among the slaves, of which many died."* – The Interesting Narrative of the Olaudah Equiano, or Gustavus Vassa, *The African*

Further, he described the inconceivable conditions of the slaves' hold—the "shrieks of the women," the "groans of the dying," the floggings, the wish to commit suicide, how those who somehow managed to drown themselves were envied. (KERA TV: People and Events – Olaudah Equiano, 1745–1797, PBS)

## Post-Traumatic Slave Syndrome

According to Dr. Joy DeGruy, the psychological trauma of slavery is ever-present in our society. As a result of centuries-long enslavement and rape, subsequent systemic racism and lynching, persistent oppression and disenfranchisement, descendants have adopted behaviors that, while initially may have had positive and necessary elements, have detrimentally lingered and manifest in a myriad of maladaptive ways. [1]

## Manifestations of Trauma for Generations

It is widely known that underrepresented groups have worse health outcomes, lower life expectancy, and higher infant mortality than whites. Even when issues such as socioeconomic status, access to healthcare, educational level, and lifestyle controls are considered, the rates of mortality and morbidity for non-whites are higher.

## Infant Mortality

Infant mortality is used as a marker of overall health status of a country. The United States spends more on healthcare than any other country on Earth, but this marker of health and societal development ranks 25th. When the infant mortality rates of white women are considered in isolation, the numbers are similar to other developed world nations. However, Black women's infant mortality rates are up to 10 times that of whites in some areas of our country. [2, 3]

It is known that chronic stress negatively impacts physical health. Some common conditions that develop include high blood pressure, cardiovascular disease, obesity, and complications of pregnancy. This chronic stress contributes to infant mortality—even though the baby is no longer in the mother's body, the effects of her lifetime of stress continue to adversely impact him/her.

The infant mortality rate for Black babies is twice that of white babies (and as mentioned up to 10 times that in some parts of the United States). Additionally, the death rate for Black children under five ranks close to that of Thailand or Libya, both developing countries. [4, 5] It was initially thought that the disparity was due to genetics or social situations, such as poverty or lack of access to prenatal care. However, it is being revealed that institutional racism is a huge contributing factor. Further, this phenomenon is not seen in women of African descent who are not American. Therefore, it is something about being a Black American descendent of African slaves that exacerbates these bad outcomes.

### Sickness and Early Death

While infant mortality is one adverse health marker that disproportionally befalls Black Americans, the rates of heart disease, diabetes, asthma, autoimmune, and many other inflammatory diseases are very prominent in communities of color. The cause of this is multifaceted and ranges from skepticism of the medical establishment in the wake of past and ongoing medical experimentation on people of color, which causes apprehension and hesitation in following recommended medical advice; to the unavailability of health and wellness services in communities of color. Systemic environmental racism, where toxic, unhealthy, and undesirable treatment plants placed in communities of color contaminate land and water supplies and pollute the air causes many adverse health problems for members of those communities. However, it is believed that the "cumulative wear and tear on the body's systems owing to repeated adaptation to stressors" [6] caused by systemic racism over lifetimes contribute to the development of ill health and early death in Black Americans.

## The Culmination

Understandably, as a result of these historical events, Black suspicion of the United States government and the institutional systems therein are justified. Ongoing revelations and demonstrations of disparate and racist treatment of people of color within the criminal justice system are commonplace through social activism. Movements such as Black Lives Matter and Say Her Name highlight the imbedded racism within American institutions. Healthcare disparities and environmental injustices are ever-present. Black Americans remember the Tuskegee experiment when 600 Black men were unknowingly experimented on and treatment for Syphilis was withheld to "see how they would die."*

---

* The Tuskegee Study of Untreated Syphilis in the Negro Male was a study that involved about 600 Black men. The study was conducted not just without providing informed consent, but the men were intentionally misled and lied to about what they were undergoing. As the men started getting very sick with debilitating symptoms, they were not offered the widely known, effective penicillin treatment. The study lasted for 40 years during which time the men

Black Americans also remember the FBI attack on Dr. Martin Luther King and Malcom X, and the systematic dismantling of the Black Panther movement, all which further fueled the belief of a conspiracy. Today, it remains a commonly held belief that AIDS was a disease created by our government in a genocide attempt, which further serves to keep Black people out of doctors' offices and avoid injections such as flu vaccinations and insulin injections.

It is no wonder that Black Americans are skeptical of governmental institutions in the United States, of which education is one of the largest. It is wise to study options therein with a critical eye and disengage when it proves beneficial to the well-being of your child and family.

---

spread the disease to their intimate contacts unknowingly. In 1972, public outcry forced an end to the study. The last widow receiving reparation died in 2009. CDC U.S. Public Health Service Syphilis Study at Tuskegee. https://www.cdc.gov/tuskegee/timeline.htm

# Chapter 2: Being a Child

## Disempowered, Undervalued, and Maintaining Control of Their Spirits

*"For several thousand years, education of children was to a considerable degree, a matter of squashing their willfulness in order to make them good laborers. A good child was an obedient child."* – Peter Gray PhD (A Brief History of Education, *Psychology Today*)

For most of human history, survival depended on skillfully foraging for food. Hunter-gatherer societies date back over two million years with the early hominins of Africa, with increasingly sophisticated tools continuing through the prehistoric humans. Modern humans, Homo sapiens, date back about 200,000 years, and archaeologic evidence shows that modern humans were hunter-gathers until about 10,000 BCE, at which time permanent agricultural societies developed.

In a hunter-gatherer society, children are active. They learn the necessary life skills to survive and thrive in their societies via apprenticeship-like work—going out with knowledgeable adults and learning at their sides. While it may seem like hunting-gathering is a simple, easy-to-learn process, it actually requires extensive knowledge about flora and fauna, weather, geography, use of fire, development of tool-making skill and discernment in hunting.

As more human societies transitioned to agriculture-based lifestyles, land accumulation became prominent. Owning land allowed landowners to essentially control non-landowners since survival depended on agriculture and domestication of animals. As those that did not own land became more dependent on landowners, the exploitation of humans by other humans accelerated. Servitude and slavery became common, and caste systems were established. Few people accumulated vast amounts of wealth, manipulating and controlling other humans.

To maximize profits and keep costs down, it was common practice to essentially enslave children—pay them minuscule amounts of money for long hours of work in horrible working conditions. It was important to keep the poor servants under control, so societies became very hierarchal. Additionally, it was essential that children learn obedience; therefore, any tendency to independently think was beaten out of them. They were to respect authority unchallenged. They were only to be taught what they needed to know to do the job they were enslaved to perform.

This human phenomenon was repeated around the world as societies transitioned from hunter-gathers to agricultural-based civilizations. Landowners were among the few elite members of society, whereas the majority of people were servants in some capacity. To keep everyone "in their places," children were brainwashed and oftentimes literally beat into submission so they would grow into their expected roles without much resistance. **America is no exception.** With the rise of industry, children were moved from the fields to the factory with even worse conditions. Exploitation of children continues to this day.

# Chapter 3: Being a Black Child in America
## Economic and Environmental Injustices and Negative Stereotypes

*"The findings suggest the suicide rate is roughly two times higher for Black children compared with white children of the same age group. These results were observed in both males and females.*

*"Gaining an understanding of these and other contributing factors may someday lead to targeted, culturally sensitive interventions and help reverse the trend in suicide rates in the U.S."*

– Jeffrey Bridge and Lisa Horowitz (Age-Related Racial Disparity in Suicide Rates Among U.S. Youth, *JAMA Pediatrics*)

Schools represent a community. Social ills that plague a community will affect the schools. Oftentimes, academic performance of a school or student is adjudicated based on metrics taken out of context. The school is not separate from the community and issues cannot be resolved without considering the multifaceted causes and contributors. Let's discuss three areas that directly affect school performance:

- Economic injustice and the negative impacts that poverty has on health and opportunity jeopardizes the family structure, leading to a myriad of issues ranging from single-parent households to drug use, violence, incarceration, and early death.

• Misrepresentation in the media that perpetuates negative stereotypes that create negative biases, microaggressions, and discrimination against Blacks, and breeds self-hate and hate of culture and community by Blacks.

• Environmental injustice and the toxic environments that prevent thriving and exacerbates health problems of the people living in these communities. Further, Black children are frequently relegated to these de facto segregated areas via decades-long practices of racism, redlining, and the inability to accumulate wealth and invest in their communities and schools to the same degree as whites.

## Economic Injustice

In 2016, 36% of Black children under five lived in poverty—over one-third. This is the largest percentage of any group of children living in poverty with a close second being Native Americans at 32.7%. Compared to white children in the same category at 11%, it is clear that there are stark discrepancies between the races in access to basic resources to live a productive life beginning in the earliest stages of childhood. [1]

Poverty has many negative implications and persistent negative impacts on life outcomes. Poor academic performance, chronic health problems, mental health issues, criminal behavior, drug addiction, violence, dysfunctional family relationships, and well-being of community are all attributable to the economic status of individuals therein.

The ability to have the creative energy, the developed intellectual ability, and the physical and mental health to effect positive change in one's life, or in their families and communities, is largely determined by their life circumstances and access to financial resources. It has been determined that the chronic stress of poverty affects school readiness and a child's ability to concentrate and do well in school. Underresourced schools are unable to meet the most basic educational needs of their students. Poverty tends to be multigenerational, affecting future generations' ability to escape the cycle.

Poverty can adversely affect social behavior in students, and poor children are at increased risk of engaging in smoking, drug use, and early sexual activity. Poor communities tend to have a high number of liquor stores and lower numbers of healthy food choices or safe exercise areas. Access to medical care is diminished. And finally, poverty diminishes life expectancy. [2, 3]

Unfortunately, due to a multitude of historical actions and systemic racism commencing with immigration and subsequent colonization of native lands by Europeans, people of color tend to make up the largest cohort of those in poverty. Some of these reasons stem from the degradation of the family by inequitable treatment and prosecution in the criminal justice system.

The contribution of disparate prosecution and treatment within the criminal-justice apparatus cannot be understated with regard to poverty and community. Even though our government actively worked to dismantle the Black community in various ways, one huge ongoing contributor was the [allowing of the] infusion of drugs into Black communities [4, 5, 6, 7] and subsequent inequitable prosecution of Black drug offenders. [8] Additionally, in prosecuting Black men, players in the system made tons of money as their for-profit prisons made many people wealthy, including the "kids for cash" scandal where judges made millions for locking up Black youths. Even policy makers and elected officials have been found guilty in participating in underhanded abuses and manipulation of for-profit prisons for personal gain. [9, 10, 11]

> *"Mass incarceration on a scale almost unexampled in human history is a fundamental fact of our country today — perhaps the fundamental fact, as slavery was the fundamental fact of 1850. In truth, there are more Black men in the grip of the criminal-justice system — in prison, on probation, or on parole — than were in slavery then. Over all, there are now more people under 'correctional supervision' in America — more than six million — than were in the Gulag Archipelago under Stalin at its height."* – Adam Gopnik (The Caging of America, *The New Yorker*)

Further, the process of white wealth-building by shackling Black men destroyed the men. Not only did drug addiction and violence increase, after serving their time, ex-felons were essentially completely disengaged and disenfranchised from larger society. In destroying the men, the ill effects on the family reverberated throughout the community and manifested as increased crime and violence, furthering poverty, and played into negative stereotypes that perpetuated the continued devaluation of Black human life in the eyes of a racist America. This single phenomenon of dismantling of Black communities and disproportionally imprisoning their men played a huge role in the ongoing struggle and disenfranchisement we see today in Black communities.

It's interesting to note that, currently, an opioid crisis [12] has been declared, a rise in mental illness has been noticed, and a subsequent increase in violence is being seen in white men. [13,

14] However, when Black people were disproportionally addicted to crack, there was no declaration of the necessity to mobilize national resources to help support and treat the problem. Opiate addictions and/or prescription medication abuse is actually of higher prevalence than illicit drug use. [15] To obtain prescription medications, the user must engage in behaviors that are illegal themselves to get the drug. And in so manipulating the healthcare system to maintain their addiction, true chronic pain sufferers and patients with acute painful illness often do not get adequate treatment or the relief they need. Therefore, prescription drug abusers actually adversely affect society to a larger degree than the crack addict because the they are manipulating a healthcare system which ultimately affects everyone. However, it is the petty marijuana peddler, or the crack user, that is targeted for crime and jailed. Now with the prevalence of white drug use, we are told it's an "illness" that deserves compassion and rehabilitation. Imagine how Black communities might be different if crack use was seen as an illness and marijuana distribution as a business opportunity.

## Misrepresentation and Perpetuation of Negative Stereotypes

Most Black people in America are not poor. In fact, white people without a college degree are the largest class of adults lifted out of poverty by safety-net programs such as Temporary Assistance for Needy Families (or welfare) and Supplemental Nutrition Assistance Program (SNAP or food-stamp program). [16] However, the media will have you believe otherwise with their inaccurate portrayals of Black people and families.

*"The dearth of proper racial representation in newsrooms is not accidental and plays a large role in the misrepresentation of Black communities."* – Sam Schwarz (Most Black People Aren't Poor, But the US Media Tells You Otherwise, *Newsweek*)

According to Color of Change, the nation's largest online racial justice organization, the media overwhelmingly depicts Black people as poor welfare recipients with absent fathers who are all criminals, [17] while white families are represented as the portrait of stability. However, it has been shown that actually it is Black fathers that are more involved with their child's day-to-day rearing, such as bathing, dressing, feeding, transporting, and helping with homework, than white fathers. Further, news and media depicted that Black people were more violent, dysfunctional, and engaged in criminal behavior, but the numbers show that whites make up 77% of those arrested for criminal activity. [18]

News coverage that is damaging and perpetuates negative stereotypes leads to implicit and explicit biases. This breeds contempt, hate, fear, and ultimately culminates in outward demonstrations of violence and racism. What American children watch on television and ingest via the media is very harmful. If one pays attention, racist undertones can be detected in most programs designed for children. Whether it is being diminished to a stereotype or subconsciously fed, it's the idea that villains are "those people" with "funny accents" and different ways of dressing. The "white person saves the day" is ever so present that it is expected and normal, which is why when a storyline deviates from the tired old racist themes and character assignments, it's indeed a big deal but remain few and far between. [19]

If your child enjoys movies like Frozen, Rio, Aladdin, or The Lion

King they are being infused with unconscious biases that chip away at their sense of belonging within rungs of an American society. [20]

*"We tend to portray villains as more likely to be active during nighttime and to don Black clothing. Similarly, our heroes are often associated with daytime and lighter colors. These mental associations between color and morality may negatively bias us against people with darker skin tones."*
– Daisy Grewal (The Bad is Black Effect, *Scientific American*)

### Environmental Racism, Environmental Injustice, and Redlining

The Federal Housing Administration created a policy in 1934 that lasted until 1968 whereby home loans for white people were guaranteed, but the policy explicitly prohibited loans for Black people, or in Black neighborhoods. Therefore, investment in Black communities was almost impossible, and Black people could not move to better places with more amenities that enhanced life. Worse, the areas where Blacks could live were mapped out and were in "undesirable" places. The effects are seen today when one compares redlining maps to current Google maps and analyzes where the "nice areas" are and the "ghettos" remain. [21, 22]

In 1968, just 50 years ago, the Fair Housing Act was introduced, which banned discriminatory lending based on race, sex, religion, nationality, or disability. This means that most of our Black grandparents, parents, and even many of us were directly affected by redlining and were essentially "trapped" in poor neighborhoods until very recently. [23]

While some integration progress has been made in the last 50 years, data continues to demonstrate that schools are more segregated today than they were in the 1970s, with schools serving Black and brown students typically underresourced with less experienced teachers. [24] Also, there is the element of "white flight," whereby white people flee an area or neighborhood as diversity increases. In instances where Blacks move into white suburbs in pursuit of the American dream:

> *Data shows that as minorities move into suburbs, white families are making small and personal decisions that add velocity to the momentum of discrimination. They are increasingly choosing to self-segregate into racially isolated communities — "hunkering down," as Lichter likes to call it — and preserving a specific kind of dream.*
> – Alvin Chang (White America is Quietly Self-Segregating, Vox)

It has been well established that communities of color hold more than their share of the toxic burden on behalf of the collective whole. It is common for minority communities to have industrial plants and toxic soils and to be near freeways, railways, and under airport flight paths that dump jet fuel into the air. Further, public infrastructure is ill-maintained while unpenalized and rampant corruption at the top levels of municipal governments have led to many adverse outcomes. For every prominent high-profile incident like Katrina or Flint, Michigan, there are thousands that never make it to television or social media.

It is important to understand that environmental toxins play a huge role in brain development, behavior, intelligence, cardiovascular disease, obesity, diabetes, asthma, cancer, and life expectancy. In communities where lead is found in the soil and/or water, IQ scores are lower and academic performance suffers. It has been shown that lead exposure can lead to increased criminal tendencies and learning disabilities such as ADHD.

Lead is only one concern. There are hundreds of harmful chemicals and many known carcinogens emitted from refineries, waste dumps, petrochemical plants, landfills, power stations, and waste-treatment plants. Decades of racist housing policies has put minorities in close contact with these damaging environmental elements.

## The Plight of [Some] Privilege and the Lack of Strong Cultural Identity and Community

Also noteworthy is the known protective effect and prolongation of life in individuals that belong to supportive communities.

In his book, *Outliers*, Malcolm Gladwell walks through how important community, sense of belonging, social justice, and cultural pride are to human health. To determine health and encourage longevity:

> *"You had to look beyond the individual. You had to understand what culture they were a part of, and who their friends and families were... You had to appreciate the idea that community — the values of the world we inhabit and the people we surround ourselves with — has a profound effect on who we are."* – Malcolm Gladwell (*Outliers: The Story of Success*)

Being isolated in neighborhoods and communities as the only family of color and being the "only Black kid" in school brings with it other sets of problems. Additional disparate treatment by law enforcement coupled with being ignored or seen as criminals by white neighbors, microaggressions, subtle racism, implicit biases among community members, and the pressure of feeling like they have to represent the entire race well to diminish stereotypes, carries a heavy burden with a large price tag on psychological and physical health.

The plight of children compounded with the racism of society against people of color results in a particularly harsh reality for Black children. Affluence is protective in many cases against many social ills. However, there is one area where being wealthier is detrimental—mental health. Rates of depression are higher in Black children that are more affluent. [25] It is suspected that this may stem from feeling socially ostracized and misunderstood. This is compounded by the pressure and anxiety to represent their entire race well to prove that they aren't a stereotype when they are the super minority in their school environments. This struggle is exacerbated today because so many people have the false belief that racism is over so the children suffer in silence with little validation.

To preserve the sense of community and enhance quality of life, many affluent Black families still live in poorer areas than white people with less wealth. [26] This demonstrates that segregation, even today, is fueled by race more than socioeconomic status. And when middle class and upper class Blacks move to white neighborhoods, they face a myriad of additional stressors that are often underappreciated but nonetheless affect school performance, family relationships, and life outcomes.

# Chapter 4: Being Black and Tested
## Stereotype Biases and Standardized Testing

*"Researchers found that the physiological response to race-based stressors—be it perceived racial prejudice or the drive to outperform negative stereotypes—leads the body to pump out more stress hormones in adolescents from traditionally marginalized groups. This biological reaction to race-based stress is compounded by the psychological response to discrimination or the coping mechanisms youngsters develop to lessen the distress. What emerges is a picture of Black and Latino students whose concentration, motivation, and ultimately, learning is impaired by unintended and overt racism."* – Melinda Anderson (How the Stress of Racism Affects Learning, *The Atlantic*)

It is widely known and accepted that current methods of standardized testing are poor indicators of intelligence, academic capability, career success, or lifetime contributions to humanity. Performance factors vary widely, are multifaceted, and to a large degree depend on home-life stability, financial security, and cultural or family values and points of investment.

It has been widely assumed that genetic differences between various races account for the disparity in academic performance. More progressive postulations incorporate cultural aspects but stop short of fully acknowledging all of the cultural components that play a role. It is assumed that there is something inherently "wrong" with "Black culture," which explains the performance difference. However, since Black culture is not separate from American culture, this "cultural issue" is not a Black one, but rather an American one, and needs to be addressed as such.

## Stereotype Threat

Self-perception is powerful. Even though many parents of color aim to instill a sense of self-love, self-respect, appreciation of culture, and methodically unravel the legitimacy of a label, the result of a society rooted in racism that permeates throughout all of our institutions and cultural nuances yields a very distressing and often overlooked and underappreciated phenomenon called a stereotype threat.

Stereotypes are fixed, often false, oversimplified, and overgeneralized beliefs about a particular group of people. While a small percentage of members of a group may demonstrate certain characteristics, it is an incorrect assumption to extrapolate the idea that the characteristic is more representative of a certain group, or further, that even an accurate generalization applies to any particular individual. It is a heavy burden to carry to be the "singular positive representation" of 140 million people of the African diaspora.

Stereotype threats are the phenomenon of observed lower performance in marginalized groups when they are reminded of their stereotyped inferiority.

In one study performed by psychologists Drs. Joshua Aronson, Claude Steele, and Steven Spencer, Black and white college students were placed into two groups—a stereotype threat group and a control group. Each group had both Black and white students with similar specifications, and each was administered questions from the verbal section of the GRE (Graduate Record Exam). They wanted to see the social-psychological predicament created when smart students were forced to include themselves in a negative group stereotype.

In the stereotype threat group, they explained to the student prior to the exam that its purpose was to evaluate intellectual ability. This was said to elicit the stereotype that Blacks aren't as intelligent. In the control group, the students were only told that it was a lab task, a problem-solving exercise, without any mention of ability, thereby eliminating the association between performance and race.

The first group, where Black students and white students scored similarly on prior standardized exams, performed similarly in classes etc., was given the exam under the preface that it was used to evaluate intellectual ability, and the white students outperform the Black students. In the second control group, there was no difference between the performance of the white students and the Black students.

The suggestion of a stereotype caused the student to perform towards the stereotype. Children of color are often "reminded" of their skin color, and the stereotypical correlation of having that skin color with intelligence.

## SAT: The Story Behind the SAT and Elite Colleges

The SAT (Scholastic Aptitude Test) was created by Princeton psychologist Carl Brigham in the 1920s as a way to ascertain intellect and fitness to serve in various roles in the military. He claimed that based upon his research, this exam would stratify people into categories thereby allowing proper placement of people into societal roles.

Stratification and categorization was thought to be necessary as there were millions of European immigrants that threatened the privileged Nordic status. He claimed that Nordics were at the top, and everyone else fell somewhere beneath them. According to him, only Protestant whites are able to be educated effectively at the university level. This ideology fueled ongoing mistreatment of African people and allowed America to turn a blind eye to the Jewish suffering and executions of Nazi Germany.

When this new exam and entry criteria were implemented, the number of Jews began to increase at elite universities like Harvard. Ivy League Jews were focused and determined with something to prove and excelled. After "Jewish quotas" were met, there were suggestions of capping Jewish enrollment and requiring that the majority of the students each year be more Nordic and less Jewish and brown. As white people felt their privilege slipping away there were cries to change the rules in an attempt to maintain their white privilege by penalizing everyone else, even though the exam they designed to select out whiteness was being taken by all applicants.

Another point worth mentioning about standardized exams is the performance on the SAT or ACT show a positive and direct correlation with the income level of the student. So, administration of the SAT/ACT allows colleges to select students that are wealthy. Since wealth accumulation has been essentially denied to marginalized people in this country since its inception, it is no wonder that those who can afford extensive exam prep are in the privileged class and appear to be more intelligent and better prepared for college.

*"The SAT is but one example of the lingering and powerful legacy of "scientific racism" in the U.S."* – P.L. Thomas (The Lingering, Powerful Legacy of "Scientific Racism" in America, *The Huffington Post*)

Standardized testing perpetuates the very inequalities it is designed to measure. [1]

# Chapter 5: Being Schooled
## Compulsory Education and School Choices

We've discussed that in order to control people, the puppet-masters must devise a system of "willful ignorance." This is done via religion, media, propaganda, and traditional schooling. The pledging to the flag and standardized exams rewarding the "correct" thinking patterns are evidence to this fact.

After WWI, there was concern that the influence of immigrants and Catholicism was in conflict with American culture. To remedy this, xenophobic groups proposed the Compulsory Education Act. This was a law mandating that all children between the ages of eight and 16 go to public school. As altruistic as this sounds, the motivation for mandated public education was to allow the powers that be more access to the minds of the children and to incorporate proper brainwashing for better control.

In ensuing years, the idea of compulsory education flourished with Mississippi being the last state to enact compulsory attendance laws in 1918. Religious leaders saw it as an opportunity to indoctrinate young minds with acceptable religious practices. Employers in agriculture and industry saw the opportunity to produce better workers. The nation anticipated the opportunity to ensure that young citizens understood the greatness of the nation and instilled loyalty for the country into the population, thereby creating soldiers and good patriots. And of course, there were altruistic groups advocating for children, lobbying to pull them out of the factories and off the farms and put them into school houses so socioeconomic disparities could be diminished.

As parents exercised their educational options, which largely included private and parochial schools, an attempt was made by Oregon voters to mandate that all children between the ages eight and 16 attend a state-regulated public school. They wanted to control what the children learned and how they were educated. Even though the law passed, it was deemed unconstitutional by the U.S. Supreme Court in *Pierce v. Society* of Sisters in 1925. It was decided that children are not "mere creatures of the state," and parents had the right to decide how to best provide for their children's educational needs as is protected by the 14th Amendment. [1]

# Chapter 6: Being Black and Schooled

## Implicit Biases and Preschool to Prison Pipeline

When discussing issues affecting Black communities today, the historical context cannot be ignored. From the enslavement of Africans to the painful integration of schools, America has a long history of racism. Today's school system is built upon this foundation and is predictably failing Black students.

Recall these major historical events:

- Mid-1600–1885 – African enslavement in America.
- 1861–1865 – The American Civil War. A multifaceted war with slavery at its center.
- June 1865 – All slaves liberated.
- 1863–1877 – Reconstruction. Recall, this is the period following the Civil War where there were efforts to end the remnants of Confederate nationalism and slavery.
- July 9, 1868 – The 14th Amendment to the United States Constitution was adopted, which in part states: "All persons born or naturalized in the United States are citizens, including former slaves." Additionally, it says that no state can deny "the equal protection of the laws" from any citizen.
- 1877–1954 – Jim Crow laws formalized school segregation. In the southern states (the Confederacy), segregation was

required. Continued enforcement of these segregation laws persisted until 1965.

- December 9, 1952–May 17, 1954 – *Brown v. Board of Education.* The U.S. Supreme Court unanimously struck down segregation in public schools, stating that the plaintiffs were being "deprived of equal protection of the laws guaranteed by the 14th Amendment." This ignited the Civil Rights Movement.
- 1954–1968 – The Civil Rights Movement. Social movement with the goal of ending legalized racial segregation and discrimination in the United States.
- 1968–1980 – School integration peaked.
- 1970s–1990s – Whites fled public schools in favor of charter schools and private schools, which essentially disrupted integration. [1]

In the aftermath, we saw a multi-tiered educational system that became more segregated with Black students in underperforming public schools and white students engaging in other schooling options.

It has been shown that when Black students have a Black teacher, they do better. They perform better on standardized exams and increase their aspiration. If Black students have even one Black teacher in third to fifth grade, they are significantly more likely to graduate from high school and consider college. [2, 3]

*"There may also be (largely unintended) racial biases in teachers' behavior. In particular, minority teachers may be more generous with minority students, devoting more time to them and making more favorable assumptions about their capabilities... Similarly, studies based on observations*

*from actual classrooms often find that Black students with white teachers receive less attention, are praised less, and are scolded more often than their white counterparts." –* Thomas S. Dee (The Race Connection, *Education Next*)

While the fight for integration was necessary and beneficial, there was the unintended consequence of diminishing the number of Black teachers, as integration largely meant Black students leaving their their nurturing (underresourced) schools to attend white schools with white teachers that deemed them inferior and unworthy to be educated. When Black and white public schools merged, the Black teachers were fired. [4] Over 45,000 Black teachers lost their jobs as it was common rhetoric for white people to say, "I don't want that negro at my school." [5] This disappearance of the Black teacher was, and remains, a great detriment to Black students.

## Racism

While overt racism—the belief that one race is superior over another with outwardly and obvious exertion of power enlisted to maintain a sense of control over another race—is frowned upon, covert racism is alive and well.

Covert racism happens when individuals or systems have implicit racial biases or prominent negative racial stereotypes perpetuated. This is a form of racism that is subtle, veiled, and at times difficult to prove. Examples include child programming that makes all things evil as Black, and the hero white or with blue eyes. Or the "white savior" who rescues all the brown and Black people in common media.

## Implicit Biases

Explicit biases are beliefs on a conscious level that affect our behavior and attitude towards a person or group of people. While they are very damaging because it's a conscious belief, it's less hidden and easier to identify. Particularly damaging are implicit biases because these are typically "good people" that deny being racist because they have a Black friend, and they are unaware of their subconscious racism.

Implicit biases are unconscious beliefs about a group of people that affect our attitude and behavior towards them and our understanding of them. It is normal and expected that as humans, we all have implicit biases. Actually, the way our brains operate, making snap decisions and categorizing potential threats, has been evolutionarily advantageous.

Implicit biases are pervasive and even exist when the person who holds them denies having them outwardly. Banaji and Greenwald suspect that the discrepancy between implicit tests and explicit statements results in part from reputation management—people don't want to express their biases openly—but mostly from dissonance reduction: They don't want to admit their biases to themselves. [6, 7]

Typically, people hold implicit biases that favor their own ingroup. However, in marginalized groups, it is not uncommon for their own implicit biases to favor the majority group. This is typically systematically created in the social structure of a society through propaganda, media, mass "education," and religion. Implicit biases are so damaging because identifying them is difficult and very personal. Since this is an unconscious phenomenon, people tend to deny its existence, especially when dealing with a diverse population of children.

Ramifications of implicit biases can have dire consequences. For instance, in medicine, multiple studies demonstrate that Black patients get suboptimal care when compared to white male patients. Medical students actually believe that Blacks don't feel pain the same as whites. [8-10] In polls, whites demonstrate that they see themselves as more intelligent and hardworking than Blacks. This is in contrast to how Blacks see the world, where in general, Blacks and whites are equals. [11]

In education, there is a pervasive belief among educators that Blacks are less intelligent than whites. And these negative associations begin in preschool! When evaluating the same student, white teachers have lower expectations of Black students. [12, 13] And this unconscious bias of the teacher actually contributes to the differing ethnic achievement gaps in classrooms. [14]

## Pygmalion Effect

When we expect students to do well, they do well. When we expect them to do poorly, they do poorly. Welcome to the Pygmalion Effect. In short, children do better when more is expected of them. These effects can be long-lasting, extending into college completion rates, overall self-confidence, and sense of importance. Research shows that even before entering the classroom, most teachers have lower expectations for low-income students of color. [13]

## Excessive Discipline

Multiple studies show that Black students are disproportionally disciplined in public schools. In one controlled study, Black and white actors were behaving appropriately for their age, but early educators were more likely to focus on Black boys as potentially misbehaving. And in the 2015–2016 academic year in Texas public school, Black students in kindergarten through second grade were four times more likely to be suspended. [15]. As such, Black children are expected to behave in a manner that exceeds their developmental levels and are adulterized as teens, and typical age-appropriate behaviors are reprimanded harshly.

## Preschool to Prison Pipeline

The preschool to prison pipeline is used to describe the overrepresentation of Black children being disciplined beginning with their entry into the public school system and culminating in their overrepresentation in the criminal justice system. This arises from unequal treatment, misrepresentation in the media, implicit biases, negative stereotypes, racist social policies, and monetary incentives to criminalize Black Americans.

## Erasure and Misrepresentation in Curricular Content

*"Under the controversial changes, a popular AP World History course would begin in 1450—essentially the rise of European power—effectively eliminating instruction on pre-colonial Africa, Asia, Americas and the Middle East."*
– Wermund, Benjamin. (AP World History Gets a Makeover, and High School Teachers Rebel, *Politico*)

Since its inception, public school systems in this country have diminished the value and ignored the contributions of people of color in the building and shaping of this country. Standardized testing and college admission evaluation criteria further contribute to this erasure.

## Inequity of Segregation

Schools are more segregated today than they were in the 1970s, and schools serving Black and brown students are typically underresourced with less experienced teachers. This forces parents who value diversity to either decide on a less academically rigorous experience by choosing an underperforming school or foregoing coveted diversity and placing their child in potentially hostile environment to remain "competitive" academically with their white counterparts.

> *"Here's my suggestion: Let the lofty ideal of integration go. Recognize that it's not going to happen and move on. Let's pool our collective mental and political energy towards the construction of institutions that might actually be designed to benefit Black students and to undo the centuries-long assault Black students have endured as a result of white supremacist and anti-Black educational systems and structures."* – Kihana Miraya Ross, PhD (Let Our Black Children—and the Lofty Idea of School Integration—Go)

To be clear, she isn't suggesting that society should be re-segregated, but rather that perhaps educating our children in an environment that diminishes their exposure to all of these detrimental elements may yield a better outcome. This sentiment is supported by acknowledging the success of America's Historically Black Colleges and Universities (HBCUs). HBCU alumni are thriving more than Black grads of other schools. [16] If HBCU grads are thriving more than non-HBCU peers, could this also be extrapolated to include K-12?

*"The profoundly different experiences that Black graduates of HBCUs and Black graduates of non-HBCUs are having in college leave the HBCU graduates feeling better prepared for life after graduation, potentially leading them to live vastly different lives outside of college."* – Gallup Minority College Graduates Report (Lumina Foundation)

Diversity can mean hostility because humans are hardwired to feel more comfortable with other humans like themselves. As such, throwing a person into a hostile environment as they are just discovering who they are—especially independent of parents as they transition out of adolescence into full adulthood—can be very detrimental as this is a very precarious time of psychological and emotional development.

Perhaps removing the hostility that comes with being a stereotyped minority in American society at this developmental stage would benefit Black students. This can be accomplished in various ways and does not require segregation. I do not think that segregation is a good overall solution. However, it is not unreasonable to suspect that segregation is a way to accomplish this goal. Homeschooling allows the child to be "shielded" from racial vitriol during academic learning, while maintaining the opportunity to interact socially as members of society with large cross-sections of people from all walks of life.

## Being Gifted and Ignored

Studies show that Black students are less likely than their white counterparts to be assigned gifted enrichment, even with comparable test scores and other markers of giftedness. However, this disparity disappeared when the student had a Black teacher. Non-Black teachers identify Black students as gifted in reading 2.1% of the time. Black teachers are three times more likely to identify Black students as gifted in reading 6.2% of the time. That's the same rate as for white students, no matter the race of their teacher. [17]

Despite a media and educational institution that is controlled by a system infused with racism leading to implicit biases that support negative stereotypes about people of color, there is no evidence that there are inherent differences in intelligence, IQ, or other measures of learning ability among humans of the world. [18] People cannot be evaluated in isolation of their environment. People of color in America are in a hostile environment that affects their belief in themselves, causes extraordinary stress on their psychological and physical selves, and undervalues or ignores their contributions and achievements.

In summary, being a Black, erased child, lost within the large historically racist American institution in a society is a traumatic experience—particularly when that institution villainizes the very attributes and features that make your child uniquely wonderful. While whites exercise school choice and flee public schools, Blacks are stuck feeling beholden to a system conceived in racism that depends on their perceived inferiority. Further, this system aims to "remind" them of this at every opportunity—from the curriculum chosen to types of testing and erasure from history.

There is no "one size fits all" in a heterogeneous, diverse, complicated society like America. And with public and private schools failing our children, parents should consider alternatives that will allow them to transition from victim to victor. **Homeschooling is one such alternative.**

# Part 2: The What?

## Homeschooling as an Educational Option

# Chapter 7: The Homeschooling Mindset

*"Contrary to the belief that homeschooling produces anti-social outcasts, the truth is that some of the most high-achieving, well-adjusted students are poring over math problems at their kitchen table, not a desk in a classroom. According to leading pedagogical research, at-home instruction may just be the most relevant, responsible, and effective way to educate children in the 21ˢᵗ century."*
– Chris Weller (*Business Insider*)

The primary role of a parent is to raise up children who are prepared to take their places in the world in a manner whereby they are positioned to share their gifts and make the impact they were created to make. Exactly what this means varies as each individual child has unique and individual gifts and tailored journeys that they must travel to acquire the necessary attributes to be successful in this endeavor. Seeing to it that children are well-educated is a critical part in raising them well.

As parents, we realize that our child is a full person with his/her own personality often evident prior to their birth. They are not necessarily like us nor are our children like each other. Actually, it is common for children to actively reject being like other members of their families, seeing the drapings of "tradition" and "old ways" too restricting for them to spread their wings and soar to their own destinies. Children are natural learners—inquisitive and curious. Their entire lives are small social and scientific experiments. They test social norms and boundaries. They break things and uncover things. They literally learn about the world, and their place in it by experimentation.

Until very recently in human history, children were educated essentially as apprentices of life. At the heels of their parents, learning the ways of the culture and investing in the family business, they acquired the necessary training to be successful in that realm. For those that had aspirations that exceeded the abilities of their immediate family, it was not uncommon for children to be sent to be trained—essentially as interns or apprentices—with people who were better equipped to help the child reach that goal. Upper-class children were commonly homeschooled where tutors and private instructors were hired to educate the child and this was one element in being "well-raised."

Traditional schooling began as a private affair where children of multiple ages gathered in one-room schoolhouses and moved up the curriculum essentially at their own pace without regard for "grades" and "levels." It was a very independent endeavor. Additionally, since the schooling was private, the ideology of the school reflected the population that attended. Typically, these schools were very homogeneous in their philosophy (be it religious, military, or trade-based), but that served the purpose for the students (and their families) that utilized it.

In America, the idea of compulsory (traditional, public) education began in about 1850, and by 1920, it was enacted in every state. We've discussed the stage, its settings, and nuances in Part 1, but suffice it to say that the implementation of this new idea of compulsory education and public schooling was not without complications. It bears noting that from its inception, the idea of mass education was founded with the idea of controlling what the people think and how they were expected to behave. Additionally, we reviewed the inherent systemic racism that's embedded within the DNA of our country and the long, ongoing struggle and fight for equality, which especially affect how we educate our children within our public schools.

In public school, a parent has almost no control over what their child learns, how they learn it, who teaches it, or how it's taught. Even trying to visit your child while in school is a hassle, and asking permission (with a legitimate excuse in hand) is expected and often required, just to spend time with your own child during school hours. Despite a growing population of children of color, only 2% of American teachers are Black men and 5% are Black women. [1] Every year, Black parents hand their Black children off to a brand-new stranger full of implicit bias and expect that the outcome will be positive for their child. The system has parents believing that only governmentally anointed daycare providers, who are likely to see their Black or brown child as a problem, can effectively oversee the education of their children.

Many aspects of parenting can be outsourced. The education of a Black child is not one of them. The system cannot be expected to protect, advocate for, nurture, or build-up your child. No system works for everyone. However, a system that wasn't designed with diversity in mind will not work to educate a diverse society and will be very much a disservice to the majority of students. In short, it is a mistake to believe that the institution of traditional school can provide the caliber, quality, and type of education necessary for your child without your explicit involvement at all levels up through college.

While the development of curricula and its execution and delivery can be outsourced, the management of your child and their education cannot be outsourced. Relying on the public school to do everything is a huge mistake that Black parents tend to make—even those of higher socioeconomic status. Wealthier parents may pay top dollar for a fancy private school, but that investment still requires parental management, which is often the missing element. Any system will fail if parents are expecting that system to operate on behalf of their child independent of their involvement.

## The Homeschooling Mindset

The homeschooling mindset entails viewing education as a parental responsibility, not a societal one. It puts the parents in charge of seeing to it their child acquires the skills necessary to lead a productive life. This requires taking an active role and not outsourcing one of the most critical parts of child-rearing. It requires the parent to avoid trusting a one-size-fits-all institution that wasn't established for their child—believing that their responsibility ends at the schoolhouse steps. The homeschool parent sees opportunity to learn everywhere, all the time, and incorporates these lessons into the homeschool curriculum. Summers are not "off," and mundane family time becomes educational. It is finding community and online resources, creating a village, and orchestrating an entire system in the service of their child.

# Chapter 8: Black Homeschooler

*I started realizing that maybe we hadn't come as far along in race relations in the country as I thought that we had. That there seemed to be a lot of messed up stuff brewing underneath. And I was feeling very much like a mama bear. Like hey, 'I don't know exactly what's going down here,' but I'm not willing to sacrifice my child as I try to figure this out.* – Amber Johnston (*PBS News Hour*)

## Why Homeschool?

Black parents that homeschool often start their children's educational journey in a traditional school setting. Like most parents, they initially fret over when to start kindergarten, the best local schools, and may even buy houses in neighborhoods in the catchment area of "the best performing schools." Then their child enters kindergarten. While they are initially overwhelmed with all the "logistics" that are involved, they feel it's a normal part of being a parent and hunker down and organize themselves.

Initially, teachers seem very supportive offering benign shared observations and criticism to the parent about the child: "Devin is a great kid, he just needs to learn to raise his hand before he speaks. But it's normal and he'll develop that in time." The mother agrees, but silently wonders if the teacher tells every parent of a five-year-old that their behavior is "a bit of a problem" while admitting that it is indeed "normal development." Mom then talks to Devin about raising his hand. After all, she tells herself, children must learn how to sit still, right?

Later in the year, Devin is being ostracized. Kids are calling him not-quite-racist names like "Brownie" or "Chocolate." But Dad tells himself that it's just the beginnings of children self-identifying and realizing that humans are different from one another. These small, seemingly insignificant, but cumulative, micro-aggressions continue. The child begins to feel the burden after months or years of implicit biases identifying him as being "bad" for doing normal kid stuff. And the parents start to feel like their child is indeed "bad." Or rather, that their child is somehow not going to make it because of the list of things wrong with him shared at every parent-teacher conference. The parents start to view their own child through the lens of their teachers.

This goes on until the parents hear about another mom who pulled her children out of school. The story is so inspiring that the parents begin to wonder if that's what's "wrong" with their kid. That he is in a toxic environment where his gifts are being overlooked. Could there be a better way?

*Our children are being criminally shortchanged in the public school system of America... When we send our children to school in this country they learn nothing about us other than that we used to be cotton pickers... The parent at home has just as much responsibility to see that what's going on in that school is up to par as the teacher in their schools... We must establish all over the country schools of our own to train our own children to become scientists, to become mathematicians. ...We intend to use the tools of education to help raise our people to an unprecedented*

*level of excellence and self respect through their own efforts.*
– Malcolm X (Founding Rally of the Organization of Afro-
American Unity Speech)

Public schools are failing Black students. This should come as no
surprise after reading Part 1 and realizing what this entire social
system is built upon. Public schools are systems that were designed in a different era for a different purpose from how we are
trying to use them today. Common triggers that force a family to
consider homeschooling are typically related to lack of individ-
ualization and appreciation for the child as a unique individual
underscored by the hostile environment created by the racism of
implicit biases in our society.

A one-size-fits-all model doesn't work because one size only
fits one size. Even the best, most progressive, loving teacher cannot effectively meet the needs of 20 students at one time. Even in
"small" classrooms of 10 children, it is not possible to individualize
the learning for one child without wasting everyone else's time.
This is one reason traditional school classrooms are so inefficient.

Moreover, an issue that affects many Black American public
school students is the low performance and underresourcing of
their schools. Even though most Black people are not poor, true
integration of communities has not been realized. Schools are
more segregated now in 2018 than they were in the 1980s, and
neighborhoods are likewise segregated. Schools in minority
neighborhoods tend to lack amenities and necessities to promote
scholarly activities, they disproportionally have inexperienced
teachers, they tend to lack the capacity to provide advanced
placement courses, there is an overemphasis on sports and entertainment, and they experience higher drop-out rates and adverse
outcomes of the students. For these reasons, parents who utilize

these schools may discover that taking control of their student's education is the only viable option to ensure an escape from the trappings of the ills of their community.

## Wasted Time

*"The purpose of education is to make one an independent, competent thinker, one who can make a difference in the world for the better, and one who has the best chance for survival and success in the world."*

*"So much in school concerns extracurricular activities that time which could be spent on real world activities is instead being wasted in these trivialities. The effect is the amassing of students dependent upon the system and isolated from the real world." – Sofo Achron (The Unbounded Spirit, Much of School is Wasted Time)*

American public school students are in school for about eight hours a day, five days a week for about nine months a year, totaling about 180 academic school days each year for about 13 years. [2] There are a couple of points to be raised with this practice:

- Despite the long hours and many years students spend in school, only a fraction are useful, formal, instructional hours.
- Why do we expect that every single person will require 13 years of instruction to master the standard American high-school level of education?

Large percentages of instructional time are lost in public schools.

The process of herding classes, dealing with discipline problems, social confrontations, and moving from one activity to the next account for significant amounts of time. When one considers all the hours spent in school and analyzes how much time is actually spent in formal instruction, young students may actually only get about two hours of instruction a day. This is particularly damaging in subject areas that require sequential and consistent instruction to master, such as mathematics. The National Center for Education Statistics report that in the United States, time spent in formal math during middle school is 3.8 hours per week (which is about 42 minutes a day). [3]

Further, The Education Trust-West investigated actual instruction times and demonstrated that high school students spend about 18 days in an entire school year on any given subject. [4] Additional instructional time is lost with excessive standardized test preparation. [5] The remainder of the time our students are in school is spent engaging in activities other than formal instruction.

Of the hours of formal instruction that are accounted for, only a small fraction of those benefit any given student. The very nature of our stratification and categorization of students based exclusively on age (and not ability or learning style) mandates that only the average student is benefitting maximally. A struggling student is frequently not ready to receive the presented lesson, and learning stagnates as frustration develops and peer pressure incites anxiety and embarrassment. An intellectually gifted student idles, reviewing materials already mastered. [6]

While Americans may be enamored with the idea that more is better, multiple data demonstrate that more school does not mean better education. In other developed countries with better performance rate statistics than the United States on exams in every measured category, school days are shorter, and there is no homework—proof positive that time spent in school does not equal quality of education. [7, 8] Furthermore, most students are capable of reaching minimum high school graduation standards by middle school. Without the option to receive more academic challenges and rewards in traditional schooling environments, it is not uncommon for these students to disengage from school and stagnate.

## Learning Differences

While most children may be able to tolerate suboptimal learning environments that meet a large portion of their needs, there is a large number of students that will not fit into the traditional school box, no matter how convenient it seems or how much pressure a parent may feel to acquiesce to social norms and expectations. Learning differences really encompass the vast majority of students. As mentioned, every child is different, and the elements that combine to create their learning style are like thumbprints—highly unique. There are some more popular named learning differences and selected special needs that help parents realize early that they need to advocate on behalf of their child for an Individualized Education Program (IEP). But most learning differences don't have a popular name and may only belong to one single child as their unique expression of themselves, and it is imperative that parents of these children advocate on their behalf all the same.

Realizing giftedness as a learning difference is important. One area of huge discrepancy is gifted and talented identification and admittance into Gifted and Talented Education (GATE) for Black, Latino, and Native American students. Being gifted is a learning difference and requires nurturing, and individualized educational plans commiserate with other types of learning differences. Too often children who are ready to advance are held back, waiting for classmates to catch up while they receive boring busy work or are solicited to help the other kids in class. So, the gifted child is understimulated and used as a tutor to help their classmates to their own detriment, delaying their own learning and advancement.

While school GATE programs attempt to help meet the needs of gifted children, typically they fall short of this goal. However, participants in these programs tend to enjoy higher quality instruction and more flexibility to engage in individual learning. Giftedness is a "special need" that requires differentiated learning techniques to yield the best results. Investment and development of this academic talent is essential to forward progress of our country. As America becomes mostly people of color, it is imperative that we have the capacity to recognize and develop the intellectual talent of gifted children of color.

There are many areas of natural giftedness, and this fact is infrequently disputed when discussing athletics or musical talent. As there are people born with natural attributes that contribute to dominance in sports, there are likewise people born with natural attributes that contribute to dominance in academic endeavors. To waste great talent, in any of its iterations, is a waste that adversely affects all of humanity. Students with natural intellectual giftedness should have that talent developed. Developing this talent is a "special need" that should be acknowledged, celebrated, and harnessed. Many predominately white schools will have leadership and teachers with implicit biases, preventing them from recognizing giftedness in children of color. Unfortunately, many predominately Black schools lack the resources to house robust gifted and talented programs. Therefore, homeschooling gifted students of color becomes a great way for them to realize their true potential.

## A Story of Special Needs

In her book, The Primal Wound: Understanding the Adopted Child, Nancy Newton Verrier states, "What the general population considers to be a concept, a social solution for the care of children who cannot or will not be taken care of by their biological parents, is really a two-part, devastating, debilitating experience for the child. The first part of the experience is the abandonment itself. No matter how much the mother wanted to keep her baby and no matter what the altruistic or intellectual reasons she had for relinquishing her parental rights, the child experiences the separation as abandonment."

Our youngest child came into our lives and family via international adoption. She was born in South Ethiopia and arrived at the local orphanage malnourished and dying of pneumonia. Orphanages are places of refuge for children and their families in the small Kebele of Guemto Guech. It is a place where a child can be sheltered, fed, and medicated. By the time our daughter made the journey from Southern Nations, Nationalities, and Peoples' Region to the capital city of Addis Ababa, she was very weak and very ill.

We made the trip to Addis Ababa as a family and upon meeting her, we could feel her pain, confusion, and wonder. She weighed 10 pounds and she was almost a year old. English was completely foreign to her and pale skin was a novel concept. After reviewing her medical records with the orphanage physician, it was clear that child was much sicker than reported.

She was likely born premature and struggled to breathe. The formula utilized by the orphanage was retrospectively believed to be affected by the 2008 Chinese milk scandal where infant formula was adulterated with melamine, causing mortality and morbidity in hundreds of thousands of victims. She had active varicella and was very malnourished, with ongoing pneumonia despite courses of antibiotics. It was revealed that her biological parents died of Tuberculosis, and once home a chest x-ray revealed bilateral upper lobe infiltrates (something wrong at the top of her lungs where TB likes to live).

My sister is a registered nurse and emergency medical technician. As a physician myself, together we doctored and nursed this child, hoping she would survive the trip back to California. I suspect that the adoption agencies matched this child with me because I am a physician and they knew she was very sick. Once home, the child was hospitalized for a week. She was discharged on a cocktail of strong anti-TB medications that required a daily public-health nurse home visits and multiple follow-up appointments to monitor for adverse side effects of the medications.

The first year of her life was a struggle. And the second year of her life she spent here in America trying to heal. Many years later, we have honest and candid discussions about the state of the world, Africa, Ethiopia, and adoption. Our family is a very conspicuous family, and we've found honesty and open conversation a healthy alternative to shame and secrecy.

A child comes into your life as a result of a very traumatic event in theirs. Losing your parents is traumatic, even if you consciously don't remember the details. This is a primal wound.

As this child started school, it became apparent that she had a high emotional and social IQ. Being that English is her second language, her developing brain had early exposure to multiple languages, and linguistics is a gift she possesses today. However, she struggled with spatial reasoning and many of the standard school subjects. Her high social IQ allowed her to navigate this awkward social situation and essentially hide her scholastic struggles. She had an Individualized Educational Program (IEP) in preschool via the public school system to enhance our understanding as parents of her special needs and learning differences.

Homeschool has allowed us to incorporate strategies and techniques into her academic journey in a way that is not possible via public schools. For example, we can spend all day on one math topic if necessary without the child feeling inadequate, behind, or stupid. There is no peer pressure to perform better than the next child. Additionally, we can focus on Ethiopian culture, history, and geography in lieu of British literature or Greek mythology. In so doing, we reinforce to the child a positive self-image and an appreciation for her cultural contribution to the world. Her personal gifts aren't those recognized or appreciated in traditional school settings. And her complicated medical and emotional history requires frequent "timeouts" to reassess the effectiveness of any academic program. Further, we can celebrate and recognize that this child's gifts to the world are unique, and her path to revelation is not something any of us can predict.

# Chapter 9: The Myth of "Good" Socialization

"*Research indicates that homeschooled children are not being deprived socially. In a nationwide study, Dr. Wesley Taylor of Andrews University found that homeschooled children scored significantly higher than their conventionally-schooled peers on a measure of self-concept, which is generally considered to reflect socialization. Dr. Taylor concluded that the socialization issue 'favors homeschoolers over the conventionally-schooled population.'*"

"*In another study, Dr. Delahooke from the California School of Professional Psychology, using a standard personality measure, compared two groups of children: a home school group and a matched private school group. Dr. Delahooke determined that 'the private school subjects appeared to be more influenced by or concerned with peers than the home-educated group.'*"

– Bonnie and Lawrence Williams (*Oak Meadow Independent Learning*)

In traditional school systems, students are categorized by birth year and packaged into units based on this singular commonality. No consideration is given on any aspect that is inherent to the child outside of this parameter. Gifted children that may need to move at a faster pace to stay engaged and maximize their potential are shunted into classrooms with children who may have a learning difference that is better served with an alternative learning approach. Learning styles are disregarded, and interests are not even explored. Life goals, thought processes, special needs, dreams, aspirations, and a multitude of factors that make us human are completely ignored. The only determining factor for placement is birth year and proximity to a building.

For many students, this stratification model based on birth year may work well. Even if it isn't the optimal environment, they are able to sit still long enough, learn enough of the expected material, regurgitate enough on an arbitrary exam, and stay interested and motivated enough to stay the course. A few students actually thrive in such structured environments, particularly if the school is diverse and they don't have to experience a constant bombardment of implicit racism. But many students are a poor fit for traditional school. Being told how to spend every minute of their day for 40 hours per week isn't ideal for them and doesn't translate into a creative, capable, critical-thinking person with a happy, successful, and contributing adulthood.

Studies show that young people misbehave more and their lapses in judgment are heightened when they are in groups together. A young man that has great judgment and insight independently may find himself compromised and unable to connect his prefrontal cortex (which is responsible for helping with judgement and planning) to the rest of the brain to offset the emotional, impulsive, you-only-live-once force of the limbic system that is well developed long before the prefrontal cortex matures and the connections between the two are strong. Peers and their acceptance stimulate the emotional parts of the teen brain and over-rides good judgement. This is the epitome of peer pressure. Unlike their white counterparts,

Black children and young adults do not have the luxury to make these social and impulsive, peer-pressure-laden mistakes and recover from them.

Learning is a very individual and personal journey. In the classroom, it is not necessary to have excessive socialization. Group work, presentation, and peer-to-peer interaction in a focused setting is helpful and easily recreated in the community. Further, arguably learning to collaborate vertically—with people of all ages, taking on the role of leader and follower—is superior to exclusively working with similar-age peers for an entire childhood. The world consists of people of all ages, and it's important to learn how to fit into various types of roles.

Socialization for "socializing" is best done based on commonalities such as shared interests, for upliftment, as validation, for enjoyment, and for friendship. The classroom is not the ideal place to engage in meaningful socialization as the focus should be on academic educational pursuits. Actually, children who engage in too much socialization in class are often seen as children with behavior problems. And there is not enough adult oversight on the playground at lunch time or afterschool to supervise and teach proper socialization to the children. Often times, children are piled together and left to their own devices, free to ostracize, bully, and deflate each other. The myriad of mental health issues that arise from being emotionally, psychologically, and physically abused is beyond the scope of this book, but it is well known that bullying and racism are very damaging to a person subjected to this type of abuse. Asking Black children to fend for themselves when they are mistreated is removing the responsibility of protecting them from the parent where it belongs, to the child who is the victim. This is completely inappropriate and does not engender a love for self or a healthy life outlook.

In the public schools, especially more integrated, well-performing schools, Black students face higher rates of depression likely due to the environments created when one is the sole experiencer of a hostile situation. Feelings of isolation, trying to fit in to a social scene that devalues your existence, fighting for self-acceptance, and maintaining goal-focused thinking is difficult when the socialization is diminishing your inherent value. Additionally, the stereotype biases that invade our children's view of themselves play out in classrooms, as teachers inadvertently send messages that align with their implicit biases—that Black people are less intelligent and white people are their saviors. Lower performance is a result because the child is saddled with all of this negative and damaging socialization.

Homeschooling offers opportunities for directed socialization where adults can serve as role models and help demonstrate proper behavior and healthy human interaction to children. Homeschooled children tend to spend more hours with adults than their traditionally schooled counterparts and tend to observe and model their behavior. Parents can create and select social environments where their child can learn and enjoy the role of leader and other opportunities where the child can interact with same-age peers. The diversity of interactions offers learning and bonding experiences unmatched in a traditional classroom. Navigating the real world ensures the quality of the socialization is authentic.

# Chapter 10: Benefits of Homeschooling

*"Racism can be obvious, like racial slurs thrown your way, but it is more often subtle and restrained. Some prefer to call it 'unintentional' or 'unconscious bias' as though intent mitigates impact when you are on the receiving end of being dehumanised. Nebulous in nature and therefore hard to call out, racism as practised on an institutional level hides in plain sight."* – Lola Okolosie (Racism in Schools Isn't Just Part of the Grim Past – It's Hiding in Plain Sight, *The Guardian*)

Black homeschoolers are parents who have decided to empower themselves to take control of raising their own children, where the decision to homeschool is not based on religious or political views but rather an expression of self-determination. Black homeschoolers are parents who decide to remove their Black children from a system of education that is not designed for them, by them, or with them in mind. Black homeschoolers are parents who realize that there is nothing "magic" about public school, and they have decided that sending their Black children off to be brainwashed and controlled by an institution created by racist colonizers for the very purpose of perpetuating myths and stereotypes about people of color is counterproductive in terms of their life goals. They understand that trying to "fix" the system in isolation as they watch the flame dim and the self-love diminish in their child is not the best and highest use of their life energy.

Homeschooling allows a child to learn academic and life lessons in a nurturing, self-affirming, culturally celebrated, and unrestricted environment. Gone are the days of parent-teacher conferences where Mom and Dad are relegated to the sideline as spectators in the education of their children. Coming home after a long day only to spend hours of a painful power-struggle over homework as a "second-shift teacher," when everyone is the worst versions of themselves, ends. Waking up at seven o'clock in the morning to make it to school by eight is a thing of the past. Eating healthier is convenient. Family bonding is enhanced, and parent-child relationships thrive.

## Freedom

Imagine the benefit of raising a child without the overbearing bureaucracy of impersonal government making intimate decisions and imposing strict limitations on how you can parent. Taking a child out of school to travel, see, and experience the world is frowned upon by the establishment. Taking a child out of school to shadow a community leader or attend a coveted community event is not "excused." If too many unexcused absences are collected, parents may find themselves in truancy court being adjudicated for doing what's right for their own child.

## Homework

The idea of homework is noble. The opportunity to learn a lesson at school, work out the kinks, practice some implementation, and then move on to the next subject helps keep a class moving. Then the concepts covered in class are reinforced at home, which helps solidify the material and enhances learning. However, multiple studies have demonstrated that homework is useless. More than about 20 minutes worth becomes detrimental, as it begins to interfere with the other more important life lessons that happen outside of the classroom walls or schoolyard. Additionally, parent-child adversarial roles are created, which typically culminate in yelling matches and tears. To avoid the confrontation, it is not uncommon for parents to simply do their child's assignments and projects to maintain peace and sanity in the home. With homeschoolers, the concept of "homework" is a non-starter because any additional practice the child needs is simply incorporated into their tailored and modifiable curriculum.

## Health and Wellness

Children of various ages need different amounts of sleep. As they approach adolescence, they require more sleep to maintain maximal physical and mental health. Chronic sleep deficits contribute to anxiety, depression, and a host of behavioral and performance problems. These problems are cyclic, with one contributing to the other. For instance, sleep deficit contributes to poor school performance. A bad grade on an exam causes the child to feel more anxious to perform better on the next exam. Chronic anxiety contributes to depression. And depressed teens tend to disconnect from their families and exhibit behaviors that further strain those very important relationships.

Social stressors, including the obscene amount of preparation necessary for elite college admission contention, further contribute to anxiety. In medicine, we are seeing skyrocketing rates of pediatric and adolescent mental illness and suicide. Additionally, the standard American diet of processed foods, sugar, and toxins adversely affects physical health and performance ability of our children. Obesity and metabolic syndrome disorders (such as diabetes, hypertension, and heart disease) are affecting our children at increasingly higher rates. Combined, these physical, mental, and psychologic stressors are taking a toll on quality of life and the overall happiness of our children.

Homeschooling allows for better surveillance of signs and symptoms of stress. Parents are better able to monitor emotional and physical struggle and intervene sooner. Eating at home allows for ready access to a nutritious and healthy diet. The ability for the child to decompress, get enough sleep, and disconnect from the barrage of teen pressure, including social media and constant broadcasting, is a huge benefit of homeschooling. And being grounded by a loving family at home supports a lifestyle of physical, mental, psychological, and spiritual health that enhances learning.

### Tailored Curriculum

Homeschooling parents have the ability to tailor the learning experience and the curriculum used to best suit the individual child—incorporating cultural appreciation, self-love, spiritual practices, family values, and academic topic areas that are of interest to the child. Time can be taken to focus on one or two areas at a time if that creates more success for the child. Strong areas of passion and performance can be accelerated. Deeper investigation and more time spent learning about areas of interest are encouraged. Areas of weakness can be remediated in a safe, nonjudgmental environment and be brought up to a level of competence. Time can be incorporated into the day for nonacademic activities such as music or athletics. And talents can be developed without compromising family time or sanity. In future chapters, we will explore various curriculum options, what a typical homeschooling day may look like, and information about vetted materials and tools that we've found useful will be shared.

## Flexibility

Grades and what a human child needs to know by a certain age are arbitrary. We buy into the concept of grade levels because that's our experience in education. However, in this technological revolution, acquiring facts and figures is not educational and is actually a waste of time. The world needs creative minds that have the ability to critically think and problem solve. Common school curricula and the methods used to evaluate competency are outdated and ineffective in determining or creating critical thinkers. Having the ability and flexibility to make adjustments that encourage their child to develop his or her gifts allows the parent to create an environment of enthusiastic learning.

## Testing

It is common knowledge that standardized testing does not create scholars; nor do standardize test scores predict life success. Many people make lots of money creating and administering standardized tests. Public schools are enamored with the idea of standardized testing to a degree that is detrimental to the children. The entire academic year is spent doing test prep with very little creative control allowed by the teacher to teach lessons that may be more relevant or better learned via an alternate mechanism. If a child doesn't get a certain score, a year's worth of classroom work is for naught, as they may not be allowed to progress to the next grade level if scores are too low. This creates a huge amount of stress for both parents and children, especially at younger ages. We will discuss later situations where, as a child approaches high school, the homeschooling parent has the option of strategically utilizing standardized exams to assess college-readiness or enhance college applications.

## Safety

Any major shifts in political ideology or philosophic expression in a society creates ripples with far reaching effects. For every action, there is an equal and opposite reaction. The election of President Obama was a legitimizing event for many Black Americans, as his election was a manifestation of the idea that Black Americans are able to reach the highest status in our society. The election of Trump was the opposite reaction that Newton promised. As society reverberates in this space, we are seeing violent expressions of fear and hate by white people who are afraid of a changing America and losing their privilege. The resiliency of the white man is much lower than that of people of color, and they are more prone to depression under relatively minor amounts of stress. [9] For this reason, the public schools that are increasingly having to lock our children inside are hostile and toxic environments.

Some districts are entertaining and implementing "armed guardians" on school campuses with the idea that concealed firearms will promote safety. However, it is clear that Black children, particularly Black boys, are more likely to be seen as threatening and as a result, will not enjoy the same sense of protection from white "armed guardians." Collectively, these issues make schools unsafe—especially for our Black children. Homeschooled children have the benefit of learning in a safe environment, free of metal detectors and armed security guards, where they can focus on academics and a healthy exploration of their world.

## Incorporating Blackness

The mandated curriculum and focus on test prep precludes even the best teachers from broadening the scope of exposure and instruction in their classrooms. Even if the individual instructor values diversity and desires to present a wider worldview to their students, this is prohibited by school district leadership. Further, the divisiveness of our nation at this time and political polarization would predictably have parents up in arms if any mention of inclusion and diversity was introduced into the public school curriculum.

Incorporating Black self-awareness, pride, and love into Black children is of paramount importance. Studies show that Black children often see themselves as inferior, ugly, or unworthy when they compare themselves to white children. Black stories of contribution and success are erased from the history books our children are assigned to internalize.

While European history is emphasized and celebrated (British literature, world history, and foreign languages chosen), African history is non-existent. African languages, art, history, wisdom, proverbs, and geography are all absent in standard curricula. Black people in our history books are relegated to slaves, abolitionists, Civil Rights activists (all fighting from a position of perceived inferiority for basic rights) are depicted as adding no value or are often seen as liabilities. We don't hear about the Black people that fought for the creation of this country or served in the military alongside white soldiers for a common goal. [10]

In group discussions, there is neither mention of the atrocities that America has imposed around the world nor the horrific colonization practices that created the global chaos we see today. In acclaimed books and literature, Blacks take on the role of the benevolent servant or the help. The Black student carries on her shoulders the weight of all Black people everywhere, and in their white enclaves, have the burden of representing Black people everywhere—whether they know it or not or want to or not.

# Chapter 11: The Issue of Survivor's Remorse

*"One of most difficult acts for African Americans is to give themselves permission to make money. I don't mean chump change. I mean serious money. White people's money. Instead of honoring those whose enterprise has taken them to somewhere within shouting distance of white people's money, we belittle them for even daring to think they can improve their condition, as if the imperatives of Black solidarity precluded any of us from making an honest buck."* – Clarence Page (*Survivor Guilt: The Angst of the Black Bourgeoisie*)

For all the clear benefits of homeschooling, the struggle to reconcile years of fighting for integration of schools weighs heavy on some who may consider homeschooling. However, integration was only the first step in a long battle, not the victory. The purpose of integration was to improve conditions for our children to be educated with equal access to educational resources. This goal has yet to be realized; meanwhile, our children are suffering. The fight for equality must continue, but our children don't have to be frontline pawns in the battle. We must preserve them so they are able and capable of carrying on the fight until it's won. Having false feelings of victory with the *Brown v. Board of Education* ruling has been very detrimental to many Black children.

After undergoing the traditional educational process, most Black parents strongly believe that there is no better way to educate a child. Or perhaps they realize the public schools aren't working but fail to acknowledge that they have the ability—and responsibly—to actively oversee their child's education. We've been told that everybody else knows what's best for our children, and we are left questioning our very capability to parent.

Additionally, the implicit biases that are inherent in our schools affects the way many Black parents view their options. Instead of investing and believing in their own ability to raise up their children, they see the white institutions as more capable. They cannot accept that their child may be better off in a different environment because this high-performing school is working so well for the majority, yet their child is not.

A smaller number of parents just aren't willing to invest in the academic development of their children. While they may pay a hefty fee for a club sport entry or singing lessons, they do not find value in paying for outside-of-school academic enrichment. These parents fall into stereotypical roles and promote propagation of the stereotypes with their areas of investment. This demonstrates to the child, the family, the community, and society at large that the misguided stereotype, "Black people are only good at entertaining white people through games, music, and dance" lives on.

Finally, there's an element of survivor's remorse. Survivor's remorse is a manifestation of post-traumatic stress disorder whereby a person believes he/she has done something wrong by surviving an experience that others did not. There are many vocal critics that suggest that an individual parent should forego what's best for their own child in lieu of the idea that maintaining the status-quo is better for all Black children. If all the involved and motivated Black parents leave the public schools, they leave behind many kids who are stuck in worse circumstances.

Are we to leave all Black children in bad situations in lieu of pulling some out for a better opportunity? Ask parents to essentially sacrifice their child for the collective, when the collective may not be interested or motivated to collaboratively engage? What benefit is to come from that? And when one is saved, why should they be made to feel guilty? Our job as parents is first to our children. We can advocate for change in the community and nation without sacrificing the well-being of our own children.

# Chapter 12: What Does it Take?

Should every child be homeschooled? Absolutely not. Homeschooling is a heavily parent-involved labor and time-intensive endeavor. Homeschooling requires that a parent has the desire, and ability, to be the executive director of their child's education. Many life circumstances and many family situations prohibit an otherwise capable parent from devoting the time and energy to homeschool effectively, such as working and raising multiple children.

Additionally, there are children with parents who struggle with being responsible adults. There are children whose home life is worse than any public school classroom. There are very damaging environments that American children endure daily, and going to public school is a much-needed reprieve. Finally, there are often people at public schools who are very compassionate and have a wealth of valuable resources that can serve a child very well. If this is the only place that a child can receive those resources, then public school is better than being stuck in a suboptimal environment at home.

Some children require many expensive services that are not covered by health insurance. While homeschoolers are entitled to these school district services by virtue of taxes paid, it may be a better and safer arrangement for children with certain needs to get those met with the assistance of an all-day public school program. Public school systems are able to provide certain services to help special needs children at a level that would exceed most families' budgets. For this situation, public school is quite possibly the best option.

Most children begin their educational journey in a traditional school setting. Typically, parents find themselves homeschooling after a failed public or private school attempt. This being the case, oftentimes it is realized that public school is working just fine, and the child is thriving. This is a positive situation and allows the parents to supply enrichment. Why pay for someone to do, or take the time to do, something when it's working well with societal mechanisms designed for the purpose?

Homeschooling is a true labor of love when done correctly. By correctly, I mean by a person who's vested in creating a well-rounded, functioning, healthy human adult who's ready for the next level of his/her life. Parents often forget that they are raising adults—the goal is an adult at the end of this project. And our activities and actions should be aimed towards this end. This is not a project to be taken lightly and requires vigilance, persistence, cooperation, collaboration, some financial resources, and a fair amount of time.

### Money

Just like most things in life, homeschooling is easier if you have some financial resources. Struggling to survive sucks away mental and creative energy. Worrying about where the next meal comes from, or next month's rent, precludes being creatively focused on homeschool videos. Further, having the ability to hire tutors when necessary, pay for online courses, and take time off work to visit community resources like museums and planetariums are huge advantages and helps round out a great experience.

If one considers private school tuition, homeschooling is much less expensive. Actually, for the price of paying for two children in private school, it is often possible to hire a tutor to cover the material daily. And for the price of three or more children, you can hire a fulltime teacher that you select and hire. This allows you to have more control and knowledge of teaching style and implicit biases as well as enjoy the ability to have open and consistent dialogue with the teacher since you are paying him/her directly. And when you look at options such as Fusion Academy, which essentially creates homeschool at school with one-on-one instruction, that same money covers a fulltime teacher.

One thing that upper-middle-class parents tend to do is invest in an expensive house so their children are shunted to the best schools. And even if these schools are a good fit, out of school enrichment and parental involvement are required. What many Black parents fail to realize is their child's classmates at the best public schools are engaged in many outside activities, have extensive outside tutoring and test preparation, and enjoy many expensive outside experiences. If buying an expensive house depletes a family's ability to provide these expensive out-of-school enrichment opportunities, their children are at a huge competitive disadvantage.

Moreover, if a Black family decides to enroll their child in private school, the same care must be taken to ensure out-of-school enrichment. Parents need to have the homeschool mindset to offer their child the full educational experience so they maximize their potential and are ultimately positioned to compete and collaborate with peers globally.

## Time

Any executive administrative assistant will attest to the fact that keeping everything in order is a very time-intensive task. Systems are established to help with organization, and research is conducted regularly to ensure that the best practices are being implemented. In addition to running a household and a family, working, sustaining a marriage, and engaging in self-care, a homeschooling parent also becomes the coordinator, facilitator, and administrator of their child's education.

Direct teaching of the academic lessons can be delegated and outsourced. Utilizing public school exclusively is outsourcing both the administration and execution of teaching, one hundred percent. With homeschooling, large quantities can likewise be outsourced. Teachers can be hired, tutors will come to the house, and even curriculum can be purchased as a set. But the time to find, investigate, and vet the many homeschooling options requires time and energy.

## Transportation

Utilizing community resources as a homeschooler tends to require transportation. Having tutors, music teachers, and others hired to help implement the homeschool plan come to the home cuts way back on the need to travel. However, there will be a need to get the children out of the house to engage in interest-based activities with peers, participate in group projects, exercise, perform, and see the world—even if it's just their own city at first.

Transportation becomes an issue worth mentioning since the logistics of ensuring children are where they need to be to maximally benefit from the planned lessons can be difficult for a busy family. Utilizing the village you create can help decrease the burden through carpooling. As the child gets older, perhaps Lyft and Uber become options. There are also "kid taxis" in some cities and old-school hired drivers that can be utilized.

## Mindset

The key factor in determining whether homeschooling is a viable option for a family is an investigation of their mindset. Are the parents able to creatively and independently think, realizing that in the Black community homeschooling is still very much scrutinized and doubted as legitimate? Belief in self is of utmost importance for the homeschooling parent. Ignoring haters and nay-sayers and having mentors and support communities mitigate negative energy. Oftentimes, people are just afraid of what they don't understand, and the Black homeschooling parent must overlook murmurings from outsiders whose criticism is rooted in their own feelings of inadequacy, envy, or failure.

Are the parents able and willing to take control of their children's educational experience? Homeschooling demands that parents study their children, investigate curricula, find and engage in community resources, and be flexible and open-minded. Parents need to be ready to invest time and financial resources into the project and may need to re-allocate funds that were supporting stereotypical activities and branch out and explore unique opportunities. Bucking the system is the entire point of homeschooling, and parental investment is a key component in creating a better system for their individual child.

# Chapter 13: Options

*"Our Whole Child, Healthy Planet K8 curriculum guides, and our high school homeschool diploma courses integrate peace, justice, and diversity studies with the core subjects. GVS is an international distance learning school; we welcome homeschooling students from around the globe."*
– Global Village School (https://www.globalvillageschool.org/)

Homeschooling is not necessarily "schooling at home." It involves utilizing community and online resources to create an educational plan that works for your family, a plan that allows for flexibility and incorporates key elements of self-appreciation and love of self.

When over 50% of the formal education takes place outside of traditional school, it typically qualifies as homeschooling. Additionally, many private schools are actually considered homeschool, depending on the state, number of students, and their corporate structure. So, the idea of "homeschooling" expands beyond what most people think of when they hear the term.

Keeping in mind that homeschooling is a mindset, here are some popular options for homeschooling parents to utilize as adjuncts.

**Individualized schools:** There are schools such as Fusion Academy, Halstrom Academy, and Alt School that offer very personalized curriculum and execution of that curriculum with provided instructors. These are private schools and can easily cost $45,000 upwards per year.

**Hybrid schools:** These are schools that specifically target homeschoolers and offer formal instructional classes two or three days a week. Common, overarching terms include "university-model" or "college-style" schools. The advantage of this type of arrangement is the curriculum is created, teachers are provided, and the children have the opportunity to engage in supervised group projects and presentation. These schools tend to be less expensive than the individualized private schools.

> *"The immediate goal of the University-Model® educational system is quality, cost-effective college-preparatory education accomplished in a way that gives parents more time for imparting the faith and values they hold precious. The ultimate goal is that of producing wholesome, competent men and women of character who make a positive difference for Christ in the next generation."*
> – University Model Schools® International (http://umsi.org/)

**Homeschool co-ops:** Co-ops are local groups that are formed by homeschooling parents to share the load of homeschooling and allow peer-to-peer interaction in a controlled environment. Co-ops range from highly structured and based on particular philosophy, such as Classical Conversations, to very unstructured and child-led, such as in unschooling. Co-ops can resemble hybrid schools but are parent-led and, therefore, are much less expensive.

**Homeschool groups:** Homeschool groups tend to be the most informal type of gathering whereby the students and families may meet up for a park-day or a day at the zoo. Typically, the meet-ups may be once a month or even weekly, but the purpose is more social and less academic. Homeschool groups tend to be free or have a very minimal membership cost.

**Private schools:** In many states, homeschooling is considered private school. Therefore, private school can range from one student homeschooling to an elite boarding school. Because of the range and diversity of what is considered private schooling, there are many viable options within this space for exploration and utilization.

**Online schools:** Online schools are fantastic options for many students. Children today love electronics, and the combination of self-pacing, collaboration via supervised virtual chat rooms, and the option of tutor supplementation yields very positive results for many students. The best teachers in the world suddenly become accessible to the student and learning styles can be accommodated. Online schools tend to be cheaper than private schools. Also, there are often options for class selection so expensive packages can be divided and costs contained.

Parent involvement is one of the most critical ingredients of a successful education.

> *"You provide the nurturing home environment, family values, and guidance that only you can give your child. We provide the expertise, accessibility, interaction, and a partnership with parents that makes the Well Trained Mind Academy a natural extension of your homeschooling education. Our*

*goal is to partner with parents in the education process, not to replace them."* – Well Trained Mind Academy (www. wtmacademy.com)

**Charter schools:** As mentioned, by utilizing the homeschooling mindset, it is possible to still "homeschool" while sending children to traditional school. A charter school is a traditional school setting that is publicly funded but established locally and operates independently. This is a good option for families with a good, local charter school that supports their ideology and offers necessary resources.

**Public Schools:** Ideally, if a public school is utilized, it is diverse and high-performing with necessary resources to allow the students a high-quality education. However, federal legislation, over-testing, mandated and inflexible curriculum options, segregation, and racism make finding a public school that offers the combination of necessary components impossible for most Black parents. Since it is often the most viable option for most families, it bears repeating: utilization of public school requires vigilance and parental involvement. The homeschool mindset is very important and incorporating enrichment is essential. Unpacking and healing the psychological damage done to Black children is imperative, particularly when they spend 40 hours a week in environments where their right to exist is being challenged every day.

## Part 3: The How?

## A Guide to Homeschooling and Frequently Asked Questions

# Chapter 14: Being Homeschooled

Homeschooling has become very accessible and easy to implement with the internet and myriad of online resources available to you as a homeschooling parent. Many super intelligent people with highly specialized skills have taken their creative gifts, packaged them, and made them available on the internet at a fraction of the price it would cost to actually gain in-person exposure to their teachings. This is a wonderful thing because it allows your child to learn the very best material from the leaders in any industry. This is not something that can be accomplished exclusively at the local level.

Homeschooling is a spectrum. It is not necessarily a zero-sum situation. If you're just getting started, consider incorporating enrichment during school breaks. In the spring, plan a summer curriculum so you can investigate available resource options in your area prior to making the leap. Step up afterschool activities by incorporating unique and new exposures that are unavailable at school. Weekends tend to be busy for traditional schooling families, and therefore facilities are crowded. But take your child out of school for a day and visit a museum exhibit based on their interests—or your interests for them—and experience how liberating it is to have the time to enjoy community resources without the crowds and weekend birthday parties. All of this will help ease you into the idea of becoming your child's lead educational coordinator.

I started homeschooling by creating what I called Taylored

Summer Curriculum. When summer first began, the children and I set "summer fun goals," where we selected activities that we all wanted to do. They would make t-shirts as an alternative type of vision board. Typical requests were horseback riding, tennis, waterparks, amusement parks, and road trips. I then asked them what they wanted to learn, and common responses were: how to animate, how to swim, finish pre-algebra, learn Spanish, learn how to build something.

With this information, I created a Taylored Summer Curriculum that aligned their desires and requests with my ideas and created very memorable summers that were recapped before school started with a photo album, where they took their own photography throughout the summer, created the layout, and added the text to a photobook editing program. Then I purchased the book for memories and to enhance their sense of accomplishment.

As summers become the highlight of the year where the most enthusiastic learning takes place and you begin to feel like the parent you envisioned you'd be when you had children, it's easier to have the motivation to create more of this homeschool curriculum throughout the year.

Very early on, it is critically important to join online support groups. This allows you to crystallize in your own mind your purpose for homeschooling, so when things get difficult, you have your purpose readily available, pushing you to make adjustments rather than give up. Facebook and Yahoo! have many wonderful homeschooling groups that provide a wealth of information, inspiration, motivation, and allows you to talk to strangers that understand what you're going through since friends and family members can lack vision and understanding. It is not uncommon for people to fear and reject unfamiliar concepts and criticize and gossip about you for thinking outside the box. For this reason, do not spend a ton of time talking to people who do not see your vision. They will only create doubt and diminish your confidence due to their own inability to embrace new possibilities.

## Haley's Note

When my mom first asked me if I wanted to be homeschooled, I was excited. I was excited because as a self-professed nocturnist, I did not like getting up at 6:30 in the morning. I seemed to feel most alive after dinner and could stay up well into the night being creative and happy. I am the best version of myself when I can start my day at 10:00 a.m. and stay up until 2:00 a.m.

Once we started homeschooling, my already solid relationship with my parents actually improved. I made better decisions, had less frustration, more flexibility and freedom, and understood the importance of these people that I call family. Friends ceased to matter, and my strongest influences came from a diverse array of orchestrated educational and social outlets that enhanced my sense of self and eliminated the overbearing load of negative and distracting influences I endured at the public school.

# Chapter 15: Learning the Rules

Homeschooling is legal in all 50 states. However, the requirements and oversight vary. The following states are the most 'homeschool friendly' in that they demand no notice to the school district and there are no additional requirements: Alaska, Connecticut, Idaho, Illinois, Iowa, Indiana, Michigan, Missouri, New Jersey, Oklahoma, and Texas.

States with low regulation are states that have an additional step or two that must be done, but overall, the parents have the freedom to easily homeschool. These states include: California, Nevada, Utah, Arizona, New Mexico, Montana, Wyoming, Nebraska, Kansas, Arkansas, Wisconsin, Kentucky, Mississippi, Alabama, Georgia, and Delaware.

The rest of the states have either moderate or high regulation making homeschooling more difficult. For example, a highly regulated state may require certain curriculum or yearly testing. Another highly regulated state may require home visits or professional student evaluations.

While I understand the sentiment voiced by some critics that homeschooling should be highly regulated, I feel that would undermine the parents' ability to customize their child's educational journey. Children are unique and governmental agencies demanding highly specific regulations prevent parents from being able to tailor their child's education to fit their interests, strengths, life goals, and philosophies. Unless the guidelines are sufficiently broad, such that Black parents could include African studies into an approved curriculum, forcing our children to read certain books or spend their year studying for a particular assessment exam is counterproductive and potentially damaging for our children. We are fortunate that we live in Texas, which is a very homeschool-friendly state where you can pull your kid out of school whenever you want without notification. But I recommend you do notify the school so they don't report your child as truant, which can be an entire ordeal.

**Homeschool Laws in Your State**

Legend

■ States requiring no notice
■ States with low regulation
■ States with moderate regulation
■ States with high regulation

Source: HSLDA. Homeschool Laws in Your State.
https://hslda.org/content/laws/

Knowing the laws in your state will allow you to confidently ensure compliance. The Home School Legal Defense Fund is an advocacy group that provides a wealth of information and should certainly be saved on your bookmarks page as a reference.

**Chapter 16: Learning Your Child**

Oftentimes as parents, we only see our children through one lens—as their parent. At piano recitals, we cannot fully enjoy the moment because we are aware of every potential trouble spot and hold our breaths until the song is over to exhale and relax. When our children express an opinion, we hear what they're saying in the setting of what it'll mean for their immediate and distant future selves. Instead of being able to just listen, we want to adjust their thinking to align with what we think they should be thinking. This is all in good parenting and is a large part of our jobs and responsibility of raising adults.

However, now that you're going to be spending more time with your children, you can relax and loosen the grip because you have time to make small, barely felt influences that don't require actively trying to shape them in the "scrub-time" at the end of a long day or squeeze everything that really matters in life into a weekend four times a month. As such, take some time to get to really know them as people. Observe their personality. Spend time talking to them about their hopes, dreams, fears, and insecurities. You will be surprised by how sophisticated your children actually are.

Remove the rose-colored glasses and try to see your children as they are authentically. What motivates him? How do they like to spend their time? Consider reading a book about learning types, personality types, and having everyone involved ascertain their personality types. Even though these aspects of a person are fluid, just the time taken to focus on it and consider its ramifications is time well spent. The book, *Discover Your Child's Learning Style* by Mariaemma Willis and Victoria Kindle Hodson, can help you with this task.

It is often helpful to gather information discoverable via personality tests—just short tests that allow you to ask your child some questions, mark the answers, and ascertain their general personality traits. Also helpful is a psychologist's professional evaluation and report. In this report, helpful information includes learning styles, learning differences, identification of special needs, and IQ testing. Tailoring your curriculum with this information will likely yield better results and informs you of necessary modifications. Allowing students to accelerate in areas of giftedness or interest allows them to begin to see themselves as competent, confident expressions of that gift. I do not think it's important to focus on weak areas at the expense of growth in stronger areas. As such, baseline remediation is important but sacrificing the development of natural talents and gifts is not required to gain basic competency in other subjects and areas of study.

## Mom's Note

When I started homeschooling, I didn't realize how helpful a psychologist report could be. These reports can be costly, and I have three children, so I didn't feel compelled to utilize this resource.

However, after our second year of homeschooling, it was becoming increasingly more difficult to motivate and inspire my daughter. I attributed her lack of vision and enthusiasm for the requisite "road to an elite college" to lack of maturity. I contemplated holding her in middle school an extra year to allow more time to prepare for the commencement of advanced placement studies and college standardized exam preparation.

As I struggled with this decision, a fellow mother in a homeschool group suggested I have her evaluated by a local psychologist. She assured me that this evaluation would yield insight and allow me to better tailor our homeschool journey to suit my individual child. After the psychologist's evaluation, it was recommended that we consider early college for Haley. The doctor admonished that holding her back and preventing her from learning at her own pace would likely cause mental anguish, emotional turmoil, lack of academic success, and ultimately could balloon into anxiety, depression, drug use, and suicide. The rate of pediatric mental illness has skyrocketed, and the results are devastating. To maintain a healthy state of mind, she implored, it was necessary to keep Haley challenged and engaged in her own life.

Suddenly extended middle school was off the table, and we started investigating early college for her at age 13.

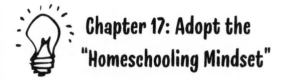# Chapter 17: Adopt the "Homeschooling Mindset"

As with all aspects of child-rearing, homeschooling is going to require your active participation. Your role as a homeschooling parent is to learn your children, then find appropriate resources that will align with their learning style and support your role as supervisor. Remember that you are the educational coordinator. A facilitator. You are not a teacher. Your responsibility is to find resources in the community or online and coordinate/integrate these learning opportunities into the lives of your children in a unique and customized way that best serves them. Your job is to pay for, administrate, and monitor the execution of their entire educational program.

This may entail finding tutors or finding interesting museum exhibits. Classes at the local public library may be a valuable component. Field trips are wonderful ways to allow full integration of the educational lessons into a homeschool plan. The very best thing about this arrangement is that you get to select the best support team for your child—tutors that you choose, curricula that you think will mesh well with your kids and enhance and foster their natural innate love of learning in a socially, culturally, and politically sensitive environment of self-empowerment.

## Mom's Note

I never thought I'd be a homeschool mom. I am a product of public school, had a great time growing up, and never had any issues in my Southern California public school. Part of the reason I never envisioned homeschooling for my family was because I had the idea that I would have to teach my children basic childhood academic lessons, most of which were not very interesting to me the first time I endured them as a child. So, the prospect of doing it all over again with my kid was very unappealing.

Additionally, I knew I didn't have the patience to sit with a child and walk her through learning elementary lessons without the entire encounter dissolving into a fit of yelling and tears. I have a low tolerance for repetition and cannot smile or maintain a calm or happy composure when a child is misbehaving—especially my own.

Then it occurred to me that the actual instruction of my children could be outsourced to hired tutors, teachers, online classes, in-person classes, and hybrid schools. I realized that I didn't have to sit at the kitchen table with my kid for hours a day redoing second grade. I could take them to a place of my choosing, specifically selected for them by me, and hire a person that works for me and my kid to do a thing I'm paying them to do. This realization was the impetus that allowed me to confidently make the leap into life as a homeschooling mom.

# Chapter 18: Align Your Resources

## Time

The most valuable resource we have is time. Planning a school year takes time, and time has to be set aside to do so. Planning should begin in January for the following academic year. Many school options actually initiate their intake process between January and March, so you want to have fully investigated these options so you are ready to act when the opportunity presents. This includes online schools, hybrid schools, and home-school class options.

## Logistics

In addition to the time necessary to research and develop the curriculum, consideration has to be taken regarding the time needed to actually implement the plan. Depending on the age of the child, this ranges from basic childcare time to oversight only.

To be a quality homeschool, someone will have to make homeschooling at least their part-time job. Someone has to be home, and invested, supervising and enforcing the plan. Children are not always rational and cannot be left to educate themselves without adult oversight.

## Mom's Note

I work from home part-time, so I am present and able to take the time to do research and planning. I hire tutors and teachers and essentially outsource implementation of my plan. My husband helps with execution by providing supervision, transportation, and back-up reinforcement when necessary.

When children are in kindergarten through second grade, their daily school work can typically be completed in about two hours. These two hours can be divided into smaller aliquots. They can be done in the evening, weekends, or early morning. Since you are controlling the schedule, you decide what's best for your family. As they get older, the time necessary to complete the assignments increase, but their ability to be independent also increases. So, a third through fifth grader may take five hours a day, but only 90 minutes requires close parental oversight.

The biggest challenge at young ages for working families is going to be the childcare aspect of homeschooling. Since the child is only engaged in two hours of instruction a day, a babysitter or nanny can be hired for less than the cost of a tutor or private school to fill in that childcare piece. If a parent can rearrange their schedule, or if extended family can step in and help cover the childcare, the logistics of homeschooling young children are easily handled.

By the time the children are tween/teens, the goal is for them to be as independent as possible. Depending on their career aspirations, interests, and abilities, they may take anywhere from five hours plus. However, this typically entails writing papers, doing projects, and delving deeper in areas of interest that tend to occupy more of their time.

Additionally, transporting from one location to another for

sports or a group activity takes time. However, these activities tend to be after work hours since most children in America attend public school until about 3:00 p.m.

## Money

There are many homeschool options that are free or very inexpensive. I recommend starting with lower cost options because the likelihood that you'll have to make modifications is high. For instance, if you purchase an online program and find that your child cannot stop opening other tabs when you aren't watching, you may opt to incorporate paper workbooks. Or the most popular math program may be great for one of your children, but her sibling may find it boring or frustrating. You'll want to change course to maximize engagement. If you spend a significant amount of money on a product, you'll more likely stay with it after it has proven itself useless.

However, I have found that to get a good product, expect to pay for it. An online class with live teachers on a good platform is going to be more expensive than a self-paced video recording. Likewise, an in-person class with laboratory experience or a specialized tutor in computer science will require financial resources.

### Mom's Note

When I started homeschooling, I utilized a hybrid college-style school whereby my children were in a brick and mortar location taking homeschool classes Tuesdays and Thursdays, all day. As an emergency room physician, this allowed me to work on those two

days, and I'd also work on a weekend day or do a weekend over-
night shift. This allowed me to work nearly full-time at 36 hours
per week (three 12-hour shifts/week) but still be home when the
children needed me to oversee their homeschool days.

## Public Services

Property owners that homeschool their student still pay local
taxes to the public school. Any special academic support services
that are available to area public-school children should also be
available to homeschooled children via their local school district
– such as speech, physical, and occupational therapy. Oftentimes
these appointments can be scheduled during the school day, and
transportation to and from the facility provided. Also consider, if
the need is not covered by the school district, interrogate health
insurance polices to understand the coverage language for these
services.

**Chapter 19: Plan Your Homeschool**

Take some time to envision how your homeschool will look. Create a system of organization to maintain control and to avoid feeling overwhelmed. Ask yourself:

**What do I want my child to learn, and why is it important that he/she learns this?** Make sure your answers to yourself are honest. If you find yourself saying, "Because it's what the public school does," or some version of societal expectation, rethink your logic. Consider that our children are growing up and will navigate a world where the job they'll perform may not even exist yet. Consider that technology in our pockets (and soon on Google glasses with earpieces) makes memorization of facts and figures antiquated and useless. Your goal is not to recreate public school at home. Your goal should be to create a learning experience designed to develop critical thinking, problem solving, creative expression, self-discovery, and broader worldviews.

**Which subjects are essential?** Humans need to be able to intake information, process said information, formulate thoughts about the information, and communicate thoughts and ideas to other humans. Formal instruction needs to be in areas where, without it, the child will have difficulty engaging in these essential processes.

Math ranks at the top of this list. Math epitomizes critical thinking and problem solving. Without formal and systematic instruction, gaining competence is almost impossible for most children. So, your curriculum should have a math component.

Language arts is critical. Being able to understand written and spoken word, and communicate the same, are key elements in being able to share human gifts with the world. As such, incorporating reading, writing, spelling, grammar, and handwriting are essential components of a curriculum.

Beyond math and language arts, what's necessary for your child to learn depends on you, your child, and the vision for his or her life.

## Mom's Note

I personally think learning how the world works is very interesting. Learning about science is learning about God. Understanding astrophysics (even a tiny bit) expands the mind and our vision of our place in all that is. Physics and spirituality go hand in hand in our household, so I incorporate a healthy dose of "fun and fascinating" physics into our curriculum. Not with the goal of creating physicists but rather to help my children realize that there is a force larger than themselves orchestrating this life experience allowing them the freedom to let go of illusions of control and try to enjoy the ride with wonder.

Some suggestions for additional topics to cover include incorporation of a fine art, such as music lessons, as there are benefits to developing brains when music is incorporated into childhood learning. Physical activity, so some kind of sport, allows the child to get out and compete, participate on a team, learn sportsmanship, and be physically and mentally healthier. Add an elective that is specifically based on their passion. So, if they love animals, maybe a pre-vet program. If they love MineCraft or other video games, perhaps a coding class.

Remember that life skills are also very important, such as time-management, self-direction, discipline, grit and persistence, resilience, and the ability to maintain a positive attitude. Also, a spiritual practice is sustaining throughout life and should be incorporated. The ability to perform activities of daily living are essential. Appreciation of self, family, culture, and infusion of self-love are of utmost importance. Being able to independently think, develop leadership skills, collaborate and build consensus, and foster healthy relationships are key components of well-adjusted human adults. Your curriculum should incorporate strategies to develop and enhance these nonacademic components.

The academic homeschool transcript can be crafted to give unit credits to these various undertakings. This is important to realize so you avoid the trap of trying to make your transcript fit public school curricular areas. That is not necessary. A better strategy is to look at college requirements and ensure that your student has enough of those credits so they are eligible to apply for higher-education, if desired.

## Have Your End Goal in Mind at the Beginning

It is important to consider the ultimate educational end goals you and your child share and strategize a path to that destination in your planning. Some careers such as medicine require a very specific path that entails recommended and required classes and exams for entry consideration. Others are more flexible and allow for more self-discovery and a commitment that materializes much later. Some universities require certain tasks to have been completed—particularly by the homeschooled student—while others are more open and accepting.

It is important to know which universities require SAT subject exams, AP exams, and appreciate dual-enrollment and unique extracurriculars. If your child desires entry into such an institution, it is important to incorporate that into the homeschool curriculum. If your child wants to pursue an artistic, athletic, or other specialized career path, incorporating opportunities to build a portfolio in that space will be critical.

## Haley's Note

I remember when my mom plotted out the pathway to, and through, college. We had an entire wall in our house dedicated to this task with various pieces of papers and exam dates pinned to it, keeping us on track. As eighth grade approached, it became clear that I needed to start preparing to take the slew of standardized exams necessary to stand out to college admissions officers. There were at least three SAT subject exams necessary, and as many AP exams that I could take. The PSAT, the SAT, and ACT were on the calendar.

Then I had to practice the piano two hours a day so I could compete at a level that mattered. I had to have a unique skill, so I worked on mastery of the harp. I did tons of extracurriculars—orchestra, fencing, speech and debate, writer and editor for the hybrid school paper. I was in two choirs, did competitive math and math circles, and I spent my summers at academic programs for gifted students.

Although I loved being busy, I did not like the end goal.

Actually, it seemed like I was wasting my time doing all these things from age 12 to 18 just to go to a college. I realized early that I did not need to jump through all those hoops if my goal was to get a college degree. The way I see it, my ultimate freedom and flexibility will come from having my education complete so I can make decisions about my life that require this credential. The sooner I'm prepared, the sooner I can capitalize on a presented opportunity. In this way, as Oprah says, I create my own luck.

## Prepare for Constant Adjustments

Perfect plans are only perfect at the moment you declare them perfect. Within a week, or a month, or maybe a year, be prepared to make adjustments to your chosen curriculum, or the difficulty level of certain subjects. Realize that every child is unique, especially siblings, and will likely resist being categorized in the same areas as his/her sibling. This can be mitigated by explaining to each child your rationale behind choosing a particular book or resource specifically for him while his sister has a different book. An instrument chosen for one child based on size or personality has no bearing on what is chosen for another child. It's all individualized.

## Haley – Kid 1

My oldest daughter really enjoys being around people. She doesn't love group work but rather working in parallel with other people—whereby they are doing their work and she is doing her own work, but they are sitting next to each other. She enjoys the energy of classrooms and learns best when she's engaged in group discussions. So, I made it my business to find resources that allowed her to learn in these types of settings.

She was in a hybrid school until I discovered she was profoundly gifted, and at the recommendation of the psychologist, started exploring early college. Additionally, I kept her busy with activities that played to her strengths, such as speech and debate and math club. She was a writer for the hybrid school paper, played the harp and the piano in the community youth orchestra, and sang in two choirs. She participated in martial arts, fencing, and attended many exposure camps such as tennis, archery, and shooting. In the summers, she traveled for academic away camps such as Awesome Math and Duke-Tip, and throughout took on leadership roles in social groups such as Jack and Jill of America, Incorporated, Teen Foundation chair, and vice president of the Rhoer Club of Sigma Gamma Rho Sorority, Incorporated.

All of this was done for this child because she enjoyed being busy. Her performance, confidence, behavior, and outlook were all enhanced when she was actively engaged in an activity that involved other people.

## Ian – Kid 2

My son is just the opposite of Haley. As an introvert, he enjoys being at home and proclaims, "It is my favorite place in the world." He does not enjoy the rough and tumble play of boys his age and feels socially isolated when in the company of groups of boys engaging in this type of very common behavior.

His learning is enhanced when he is comfortable, at home, and free to pause a video and ask a question or type ideas and thoughts in a group-chat room in an online classroom. When made to go to class, he is quiet, and his mind wanders, only paying enough attention to answer an impromptu question the teacher may throw his way.

So for him, I investigated various online courses with live interaction. Since he doesn't enjoy being busy and spends his free time engaged in computer animation or watching dinosaur videos, I encourage the self-direction and self-discovery. I do not fill his schedule with "busy-ness" and try not to incorporate an abundance of social interaction because it doesn't serve him well. While he'll artfully endure just about anything thrown his way, he thrives at home.

## Hana – Kid 3

Finally, my youngest is a social butterfly. She loves the idea of school, and if the socialization at the schools were more integrated and diversity was celebrated while the quality of the academics remained high caliber, school would be the perfect place for her to thrive.

With her, we actually started her out in kindergarten in public school. She was wide-eyed, super excited, and very eager to go and make friends. The first week of school, another child called her a racial slur, and even after expressing outrage to the school leadership about that type of emotional bullying, nothing was done. As politics changed in the country and moved from an Obama-led country to one of hate and fear, the children in the local public schools reflected this shift in their attitudes, mannerisms, and embolden expressions of xenophobia. Being that Hana is an African immigrant and adopted into a mixed-race, conspicuous family, it was particularly hurtful to her when the class singled her out, saying that she should go back to where she came from.

Instead of fighting the public school system, we opted to put her in the hybrid school with her siblings. And it was a great situation. Hana loved the school, and her only criticism was that she couldn't go five days a week.

So once again, we tried the public school at her specific request in third grade. She was enamored with the idea of going to a traditional school, and I felt it was important to investigate this option for her. She was there for a semester, and it was a disaster. Not only was the implicit biases affecting the entire interaction between students and staff, and staff with parents, repeated microaggressions were becoming difficult to explain to a child that "only wanted friends," and "no one would play with her."

What prompted me to pull her out of public school at the end of third grade was the overemphasis on the state testing. With my oldest, the testing was not questioned because there was never a threat of her not passing. My son left the public school system prior to the initiation of the exams. However, now as my youngest struggled to pass pre-tests of the STAAR, even after sitting in class all year and doing well in school, I grappled with whether or not the extra tutoring they wanted her to undergo (extending her school day by an hour or two) just to pass an arbitrary exam was worth getting her up an hour earlier before six, before the sun came up, to learn items for an exam.

Then I thought about the struggles that would follow her with regard to this exam the following year when promotion to fifth grade would be threatened. And I realized that her enthusiasm about learning was free falling as she started seeing herself as the "stupid chocolate girl that should just go back to Africa where she belongs."

With this, I pulled her out of public school and put her in private school.

Private school was a great environment academically. The testing done wasn't to hold students back but rather to ascertain their strengths and weakness to offer more individualized help. The philosophy of the school was more inclusive and being a religious school, focused on answering to a higher power. The curriculum was good, and the teachers were kind and caring. I was paying handsomely for this experience, but it seemed to be perfect.

Then towards the end of the first semester, there was evidence of bullying surfacing. Social ostrization and "mean girls" started to make my child further question her value. I am fortunate to have had my oldest daughter tell me that the youngest was silently suffering at the private school. She was eating alone at lunch or shared assigned seating with someone that didn't like her. Evidence of self-harm became apparent as she feigned illness and cut her hair off. I had a long, honest talk with her and being the ever-optimistic non-complainer, it was like pulling teeth to ultimately get her to admit: "I like the school, but the school and nobody in it likes me."

Since I was spending thousands of dollars, I immediately felt that the combination of social isolation, microaggressions and bullying, exam anxiety, and evidence of self-harm, were enough to pull her out of traditional school altogether and bring her home to unpack, sort, and dispose of all those internalized ideas of self-hate. She is enjoying homeschooling and after some time away from the drama, really appreciates learning at her own pace without being made to feel "dumb." Additionally, since there is more time for extracurriculars, she is enjoying the socialization that she hoped school would provide via community social groups, my

⋮ sorority youth affiliate group, and deepened relationships with
⋮ children in my mothers' groups.

## Curriculum Options

Specific curriculum options develop quickly and change frequently but the general themes can be categorized.

### Homeschool Hybrid (University or College-Style Schools)

These homeschool options create the curriculum and execute it with parental collaboration and oversight. This is a great option for a new homeschooling parent to gain confidence and relieve anxiety that their child will miss something.

### Box Curriculum

These come prepackaged and complete. All the subjects are packaged together at a certain grade level so you just open the box and implement the academic lessons therein. As with all aspects of homeschooling, Mom or Dad can be the teacher. Particularly at the more advanced levels, tutors can be utilized and many boxed curricula have online access to an instructor that offer student and family support when needed.

### Homeschool Classes

Homeschool classes are great adjuncts to other methods. And if a few are taken simultaneously they may actually constitute a very nice, comprehensive program. Homeschool classes can be in-person at a facility that caters to this market. Private schools often have the liberty to decide if they will allow a homeschooled student up on campus to take one or two classes. Public libraries, museums, and community centers frequently offer classes and workshops that can serve as a "homeschool class." Other options for homeschool class selection entails exploring online options. Online classes can be individual courses, or an entire program. These are great, inexpensive options for students that enjoy on-line, chat-room style interactions and have the discipline to focus while on a computer with full internet access. In sum, homes-chool classes are classes that you find for your child to take.

## Freestyle

Utilizing various methods and strategies to pick and choose the parts that best serve your family and your student is known as "eclectic homeschooling" or freestyle. This can range from a very regimented academic program to unschooling, which is com-pletely child-led. Freestyle allows you to pick and choose various programs, community resources, and put together your own com-prehensive curriculum—which may be only three critical classes. Typically, freestyle homeschooling requires a bit more confidence in yourself as a homeschooling parent. Selecting a combination of the above resources while perhaps incorporating community resources makes this option the most time-intensive and may be an overwhelming place to begin for a new homeschooler.

## Haley's Note

I liked being in class. It was easier for me to be engaged. I have since learned that I am an audio learner, so I used that knowledge to maximize success opportunities. Thankfully, my mother knew this information too and signed me up for homeschool classes that I enjoyed. It was particularly nice because the school and classes were only twice a week, so the benefits of being in that environment were enjoyed; but the distractions and drama were minimized.

### Incorporate Opportunities to Socialize

The most common issue that confuses non-homeschoolers about homeschooling is that of socialization. Human beings are by nature social creatures. We thrive in groups, live in packs, and die in isolation. Incorporating social human interaction into the lives of children is not difficult, and really requires no special effort.

However, if we want our children to have specific types of interactions, they will require focused coordination. For instance, in certain parts of suburbia, days may go by between seeing another Black family. Interacting with another Black child may require a concerted effort in order to manifest. If your child has unique interests, it's very reassuring and legitimizing to connect with people who share those interests. Similarly, having an ideology that markedly differs from the predominant belief in a community will require the parent to engage in systematic efforts to connect with like-minded individuals.

None of this is taken into consideration in the hodgepodge socialization that is public school, and therefore frequently ends up being very counterproductive, soul-crushing, and deadly. Common belief systems will have you believe that the best socialization is completely random and done while trying to master algebra. We buy into the concept that the only useful socialization originates in school and the "best people" to have our children around are crazy, racist bullies who demean our children—kids that share no ideologies with our children or family.

## Mom's Note

I came to quickly realize that the concept of socialization and kids needing to socialize with other little, illogical, distractible people just like themselves in order to become well-adjusted, responsible adults is a myth! It's akin to putting your puppy in "puppy-class" 40 hours a week with other puppies and expect the puppy to know how to behave around humans.

I'd argue that the peers your children meet in moms' groups, family, sport teams, bands, orchestras, debate camp, horseback riding lessons, robotics, etc. are more meaningful, stable relationships. Sharing a common interest is an essential element to true friendship.

Socialization also needs to be vertical, not just horizontal. The problem with typical school kids is they are not independent thinkers. Public school doesn't like non-conformity; it's impossible to teach 20 different methods to 20 different kids. To try and mitigate variances in learning levels, children are grouped in grades by their birth years. This is not for the benefit of the child but rather in an attempt to make the system work. However, our children would benefit from the opportunity to learn from older peers and lead younger ones.

Well-socialized children are better behaved and can interact with humans of all ages. They are not intimidated to speak their mind. When a child is engaged in the very individual and personal process of learning new academic material, other kids are oftentimes a distraction. When it's time to socialize, proper and supervised socialization is necessary in order for children to receive the proper instruction on how to properly behave. Throwing a bunch of random children together on the playground with no supervision or instruction decompensates to a Lord of the Flies popularity contest where poor decisions are reinforced by same-age peers.

## Mom's Note

My husband was very apprehensive about homeschooling. But I spent time explaining so I could help him understand, "We go to school to learn, not for friends." I reminded him how much more our kids will learn with a customized education. I showed him that healthy and appropriate social outlets were abundant in the community. I pointed out that overvaluing group thought and holding friends to a higher level of value than academic achievement goes against our parenting philosophy. Current childhood friendships are inherently unstable and don't deserve further consideration.

Ultimately, it comes down to accepting that handing your child over to a different stranger each year to babysit alongside of a bunch of random kids that just happen to have a birth year in common for 40 hours every week is not what's best for your child simply because there are other kids there. Neither does this make for good socialization.

Spend time seeking opportunities for positive socialization.

Select activities that are interest-based and align with ideals that will enhance your child and support your family. Some great options include individual and team sports; homeschool and community college classes; places of spiritual worship; Lego and robotics clubs; video game tournaments; poetry slams and other expressions of art; Girl or Boy Scouts; hobby groups such as photography clubs, ceramics, and painting; math circles and star-gazing gatherings; musical choirs, bands, or orchestras; and homeschool and community social groups that congregate for park days and field trips. The list expands with your creativity.

## Haley's Note

The main questions I'm asked center around socialization. Here's the thing—I never held any of those random kids in my class or school in high regard. I was very often the only Black kid. One time in a school play, they even suggested that I be the slave. During the entire unit on the Civil War (they called it the War of Northern Aggression), half the class would diminish me by reminding me that, "I would have been their slave if we were still in that era." That's how they saw me.

I also remember trying to ask secondary questions about topics the teacher presented in class and being shut down because my questions were off topic or went too far into the subject matter. In retrospect, I think the teacher just didn't know the information well enough to expand on the topics. But at the time, I felt like I was breaking an unwritten rule for asking the questions. Other students were playing around on their phones or sleeping in class, and the teacher would repeat lessons and cater to those students. There was no reward for actually paying attention and learning the information. It got to the point where I realized that I, too, could goof off and still get a solid B on everything.

It was a social disaster as I tried to acquiesce and learn social lessons from these random, hateful children. And it was an academic disaster since I wasn't able to learn at my level, my questions were unwelcomed, and I could cruise below the radar doing essentially nothing and still get a B+ on everything.

# Chapter 20: Starting Your Homeschool

## Creating Space

Think about where in your home you will organize and store your homeschooling items and conduct homeschooling activities. It's helpful to have an area in a room with bookshelves and a filing mechanism. If you have more space, an entire room outfitted complete with educational games, books, supervised computer access, desks and tables that support collaboration, dry-erase boards, and plenty of light would be ideal. The majority of learning and instruction will very likely take place beyond the walls of this space, but having a dedicated area is helpful. Also, setting up this space helps you transition into the homeschooling mindset, and this is helpful to maintain your motivation and inspiration as you navigate the other logistical and technical aspects of homeschooling.

## Make it Legitimate

Homeschooling is legal in all 50 states. Resting assured in this knowledge arms you with the necessary ammunition to persevere and find a path. In Texas, a parent only has to notify the school that the child will be homeschooled as they pull them out. In California, a parent has to file an affidavit to function as a private school or enroll in a private school satellite homeschool program.

Setting up your homeschool is state specific and will require some time to research to ensure you are aware of all your options and can defend your educational decision to others who may question (such as authorities, family members, or other "well-meaning" people who may want to get DPS involved).

Homeschooling Legal Defense Association and Time 4 Learning websites are both excellent resources to investigate the nuances of homeschooling in your state.

HSLDA: https://hslda.org/content/
Time 4 Learning: https://www.time4learning.com/

### Document

Start documenting so your thoughts and ideas are congregated and organized. Blogs are great (and can be private or shared with interested parties). Additionally, blogs can be turned into great books that serve as personalized historical documents, reference books, and even yearbooks. Blogs also allow you to link to and archive other websites and helpful groups and blogs as you acquire an overwhelming amount of information. Documentation also helps you ascertain what worked, what didn't, and helps hold everyone accountable.

### Educational Goals and College Preparation

There are many educational philosophies (such as Montessori, Waldorf, and Reggio Emilia), and it is likely that your homeschool will incorporate various aspects of many types. A consideration should be given to the type and extent of religious incorporation, which will help guide you towards certain curricula. For example, Classical Conversations is a popular option for many who homeschool to emphasize a Christian worldview. Bob Jones University and Abeka are other options. I've found these tried-and-true Christian options to have some great pieces, but as an entire holistic curriculum is lacking in areas that should incorporate diversity, inclusion, and love for your neighbor or fellow man. The prototype of the American homeschooling family has been a very conservative, xenophobic, "Christian" group, and the learning materials tend to cater to that crowd. Additionally, instead of infusing a singular interpretation of a religion into every aspect of academic instruction, it can be helpful to Black children to use that opportunity to infuse a respect for self, identity, and culture and change the popular religious messages that tend to be judgmental and presented in a way that attempts to "prepare students to defend their Christianity," which is the mainstream dogma, to one that is truly more Christ-like that incorporates love and acceptance for all people without judgment.

There are also the guidance and resources of homeschooling pioneers such as Susan Wise Bauer, author of *The Well Trained Mind*, which explains and supports a Classical Education. This is a great baseline guidebook but can quickly become overwhelming if all aspects of a Classical Education are thought to be necessary and actively incorporated into your plan. What I particularly like about the Classical method is the subdivisions of learning based on natural developmental tendencies—grammar, logic, and rhetoric. The grammar stage consists of foundational language skills. In this stage, children are "fed" information. The next stage is the logic stage that focuses on the development of reasoning. In this stage, the children use foundational information from the grammar stage and learn to critically analyze this information. The final stage is the rhetoric stage. After learning the foundational material, building on it, analyzing it, and criticizing it, they are now ready to express themselves and articulate their thoughts. Even if this method is not followed, having this guidebook and loosely following these stages allows you to find appropriate material and take it through this process all the same.

Finally, it is also important to consider the end goal of this process for your individual child and family. With the end in mind serving as a beacon, as the sea of homeschooling gets cloudy, your beacon will be a great guide. Of course, your end goal will change as your children grow into full self-expression, but there are big considerations that you can explore to get you started.

Your goal for your child should be to get him/her college ready so that option is maintained until actively and consciously dismissed. Regarding college prep, is the goal to get into an elite university or Ivy League school? If so, you need to create a plan that begins in sixth or seventh grade that is orchestrated to this end. A great resource to help you get started thinking about how to make this happen is *What High Schools Don't Tell You (And Other Parents Don't Want You to Know)* by Elizabeth Wissner-Gross. In this book, Elizabeth outlines many of the necessary hoops that must be jumped through to have a real shot at an Ivy League admission. Additionally, however, the book is full of information that is not commonly shared by high school counselors. This book is a MUST READ for any parent with an ambitious student looking to attend top universities.

All the top elite colleges and universities accept homeschool students, and many are starting to show preference for them. However, they often ask for some additional objective information, such as SAT subject tests and AP exam scores. Community college transcripts with dual-enrollment classes can help legitimize a homeschool transcript as does virtual high school classes and CLEP exams. If a student is expected to take the PSAT, SAT/ACT, 5+ AP exams, 3 SAT subject exams all while excelling at a sport or instrument and engaged in meaningful leadership activities, it is impossible to get that all in if you start in ninth grade when college applications are due the summer before twelfth. If a student wants to participate in the Physics Olympiad, he/she would have needed that accolade prior to senior year in order to put on college applications. However, most school systems don't even have a sequence of classes that allows students to be ready to compete in calculus-based physics prior to senior year, so this is something you'd have to modify. Additionally, significant research and national science fair accolades are great ways to stand out, but time to engage in these activities needs to be incorporated very early.

If your goal for your child is to start college early, you'll have a different set of considerations and likely a particular local school in mind. It is important to learn what the admissions requirements are for any college being considered so you can incorporate specific college-prep training into your curriculum. For instance, the dual-enrollment classes you select at the local community college should align with degree requirements or otherwise serve to expose the child to possible major choices and/or career options. It's important to realize that planning for a sports scholarship tends not to be a great plan for the vast majority of students for multiple reasons. Playing college sports on scholarship is a full-time job. It interferes with academic performance, and unless the end goal is a professional career in said sport (which we know the chances of that are minuscule), it can be counterproductive.

The investment of resources (time, money, energy) in

developing a "top tier" athlete is significant. And the return on that investment is a lottery. An investment of those same resources into academic performance has a yield that is much more predictable. For example, paying for gymnastics lessons for 12 years at $500/month will cost upwards of $72,000. Incorporating the leotards, warm-ups, travel, and extra training (dance lessons, extra gym time, camps, etc.), it is reasonable to assume that a significant amount of time (36+ hours/week) and money ($100,000+) has been invested into this endeavor. What else could your child do with 22,000 hours and $100,000? These are real considerations as you plan how your child will spend their time and how you will spend your money.

### Create a Village

Along the journey of homeschooling, it is exceedingly helpful to immerse yourself in homeschool support groups. As you and your family find your bearings, it is deflating to hear criticism from people who do not know you or your child and have not seen or experienced your struggle. Your child is not a hostage to their (uninformed) opinions about how you live your life or the decisions you make on behalf of your individual child and family. Therefore, to have creative sounding boards, encouragement, and sound information, you'll find online support groups beneficial.

### Create an Academic Curriculum

When you are first getting started, focus primarily on only two academic areas:

- Math and problem solving
- Language arts and communication

It is important for your child to know how to think and figure things out. And it's important for him to be able to share with the world his thoughts and ideas coherently. If young humans learn how to think and figure things out, they can later teach themselves anything. If they learn how to effectively share their ideas, they can be anything. Focus on math and language arts. Later, you can incorporate science at their level and depending on interests. Remember, nobody has to know everything. We aren't rewarded as adults for "knowing everything." Society does not expect people to know everything. However, knowing well what you know is how you make a living and contribute your gifts to the world. Focus on math and language arts, and then incorporate strategic and specific additional areas of study (but not ALL of them) depending on your particular child's talents and interests.

**For a young student in pre-kindergarten through early elementary school, the curriculum may look something like this:**

- Spending time learning letters, colors, and numbers through ABC Mouse online or do phonics using *Explode the Code*
- Engage in handwriting development with a book like *Handwriting Without Tears*
- Planting a vegetable garden with a parent
- Going to weekly Spanish story time at the local library
- Swim lessons at the YMCA or other community center
- Music lessons (consider selecting an instrument that isn't

as mainstream so your scholar will have the opportunity to uniquely stand out as they master said instrument)
- Getting age/level-appropriate workbooks in math and working through them at a comfortable pace

**For a lower elementary school student, the curriculum may look something like this:**

- Math with *Beast Academy* graphic storybooks and supplemental workbooks
- Typing and cursive writing with *Learning Without Tears*
- English grammar via Kamali Academy
- *Spelling You See Level C Wild Tales*
- Programming with Scratch via edX (https://www.edx.org/course/programming-scratch-harveymuddx-cs002x-1)

**For an upper elementary school, the curriculum might look something like this:**

- Pre-Algebra with Teaching Textbooks
- Problem solving with Elements of Mathematics Foundations
- Writing Fundamentals (with grammar incorporated) via Well Trained Mind Academy online
- *Reading Detective* workbook for reading comprehension
- Exploration time by choosing a few Ted-Ed or Crash Course Kids to enjoy (to later discuss with you at dinner)

**For middle school, the curriculum may look something like this:**

- Geometry with Art of Problem Solving online with private home math tutor support
- Writing with the Institute for Excellence in Writing Level B
- Computer Science with Online G3 (or some other science such as biology, chemistry, psychology, or physics with Online G3)
- Paleontology study (because my son loves dinosaurs) by watching EONS on PBS online
- How to Become a Super Star Student with Great Courses Plus
- Focus more on the end-goal strategy (preparation for subject exams, ACT/SAT, PSAT, and development outside of academics by delving deeper in extracurriculars and leadership)

At this time, you will want to consider having your child take the ACT or SAT for entry into the Talent Searches. Please know that an acceptable score on either of these exams allows entry into all of the Talent Searches. And your child is able to sit for these exams by simply signing up on the registration sites (ACT or SAT site) and selecting a local administration location. No permission necessary.

Source: Center for Bright Kids

**For high school, the curriculum may resemble:**

- Dual-Enrollment class of a course previously taken online (such as biology for non-science majors) to maximize success. Or an "easy" core class such as English Composition I or a core history class
- CLEP study to test out of college algebra and get college credit for it
- SAT/ACT online prep course
- Creative writing class via Brave Writer Online Essay Prep Courses
- Spanish course on Great Courses Plus
- AP Biology using Thinkwell, Bozeman Biology, Crash Course, and Khan Academy (all online and integrates nicely to offer further explanations and expansion on topics from many directions)
- Online physics courses, such as Awesome Math, to prepare for the Physics Olympiad
- Creation of leadership opportunities, extra coaching in areas of interest and talent to pull away from the herd in these areas

Throughout the year and during summer, incorporate reading materials from a list of empowering, diverse, and validating authors. Visit museums and planetariums, join star-gazing groups, take driver's education classes, private music lessons, attend interest-based camps, enter video game tournaments, and nurture positive vertical socialization. Volunteer at animal rescues such as the Humane Society or community food banks. Introduce world history and other social sciences in a setting where Africa is celebrated and the diaspora appreciated. Perhaps participate in mothers' groups such as Jack and Jill and Mocha Moms for a pool of friendship opportunities. Find a place of spiritual worship for connection to a source of energy higher than oneself and make some friends. Libraries often have programming that is relevant and engaging. Black sororities and fraternities have youth affiliate groups that also serve as culturally sensitive socialization and exposure to an expanded village.

Always keep in mind, you have zero obligation to recreate the public school that isn't working, at home. The goal is to infuse self-love, self-respect, celebration of culture, and Blackness into the educational process. This means you can incorporate methods that work towards this goal and completely eliminate (without worry of whether the student will be college ready) many areas that fall outside of learning how to think and express oneself.

Finally, ensure that you incorporate opportunities for growth and independence into your homeschool plan. Give the children as much responsibility as they can handle. Have them keep track of their time and tasks and help participate in what they learn and study, how they study, when and where they study, and with whom. Teach accountability, organization, and life skills. Initially, it may be necessary for a new student to have a parent print out a monthly (or weekly) calendar to populate tasks and times. As the year progresses, transition this responsibly to your scholar.

Much of your time as a homeschooling parent will be devoted to this task—finding, vetting, and implementing curriculum. There are many supply exchanges to keep costs down, and there are opportunities to share and split the cost of some items with other families. But expect to pay for quality materials. There are some decent and nice free or low-cost options but not for every subject and every level. Prepare to buy things that work for a short-period of time and need to be thrown out before the semester is even over. Realize that the only thing constant is change and become comfortable and okay with change.

## Time: Plan your Day

Initially, it's overwhelming to manage time because there are too many variables to make an accurate prediction. Sleep is health protective and supports effective learning. Older children and teens work best later in the day and into the evening. Therefore, allowing the child to naturally wake up is excellent. However, realistically a 10 a.m. wake-up time is reasonable, with a goal to start work by 10:30 a.m.

### Pre-K and Kindergarten

Pre-K is primarily play-based learning and happens all the time. Formal "teaching" of letters, shapes, etc., can be done via a computer program such as ABC Mouse with supplemental workbooks and educational games and TV shows. A pre-K child's formal educational time might be 30 minutes up to an hour a day. They will learn plenty with that one-on-one focused attention a few days a week. As they enter kindergarten, increase the time to about 60 to 90 minutes.

### Lower Elementary School

As the child enters into elementary age, total school time increases. Grades first through third may be about three hours. I've found that it's helpful to allot a least two hours to math—it always seems to take longer than anticipated.

Allow for movement, snacks, and breaks but ensure that they don't become distracted for prolonged periods of time. Many young students up until about third grade require close supervision because they tend to get distracted without close oversight. A good strategy is to give them their entire "list of things to do today" with check boxes that they can check once the task is done. This sets them up to organize their own time later on in the process. After they've spent what seems like an appropriate amount of time on a subject—or after about 45 minutes—get up and check their progress. Make corrections and provide instruction. Then move on to the next topic. Not all subjects need to be done each day. If a concept in math is particularly difficult and takes three hours, save writing for the next day (or the next week).

## Upper Elementary School

From about fourth grade through sixth grade, the child will likely be able to go through his entire list of "things to do" within a reasonable time (3-4 hours). If it's taking way longer than that, perhaps the material is too difficult, or there is too much of it. If the child is motivated by "getting things done," reward that initiative with free time (don't penalize it with more work). If the child is consistently getting all the work done in one or two hours, make the work more difficult (go to the next level) or add another subject (even if it's a "fun" subject like Coding with Minecraft).

## Middle and High School

Over sixth grade, the child should be able to complete all work timely and should be trusted to check and correct their own work. Exam administration is helpful to ascertain their academic honesty, and exams are typically incorporated into the online classes, workbooks, or easily created using many online tools. From about sixth grade onward, the amount of time required to complete tasks varies depending on the goals of the child and family. Reasonable amount of time engaged in schoolwork is about five hours. With breaks and distractions, it's easy to go from 10 a.m. until about 4 p.m. or 5 p.m. But then, they stay up late engaged in interest projects until midnight or so. Of course, there may be sports practice, social outings, music lessons, etc., that requires an older student to come home from those activities and complete assignments.

What they study and how they spend their days depends on their end goals, interests, your plans for them, available options and resources, and family dynamics. For example, if instead of British literature you'd like your child to learn African proverbs and ancestral wisdom, you are able to make that substitution. If their goal is to participate in academic competitions such as the U.S. Physics Team, American Mathematics Competitions, or the Biology Olympiad, much of their time and your focus will be on finding and providing resources that will enhance skills and performance in these areas. As homeschooled students, they are at a distinct advantage because they are able to dedicate time and resources to these endeavors that traditionally schooled students would find more difficult to manage.

If the motivation for homeschooling is to condense instruction time to allow for engagement in time-intensive specialized training (such as elite athletics, young students that work full time perhaps in entertainment, or students in families that travel frequently), asynchronous (recorded) lessons with teacher access via email and telephone may prove most useful. Private tutors can still be hired, and interact with the student online, if necessary, to help answer questions and explain lessons. A student in this situation will have a day that looks quite different from a student attending a part-time, in-person hybrid school.

There are online schools that are excellent and very highly rated, such as Stanford Online High School. There are online schools that are excellent and allow for parental execution such as Oak Meadow and Global Village School. Locally, there are "university-model" or "college-style" schools that offer a two or three day a week option of homeschool classes where the remaining days of homeschooling incorporate a selection and administration of the curriculum in which parents simply supervise. The great thing about these options is that it is typical for parents to have ultimate oversight and be intimately involved in awarding credit and selecting areas of participation. Additionally, some private schools will allow a homeschool student to take classes, participate in extracurriculars, or otherwise utilize their systems (for a fee). And some public school districts mandate this availability to area students.

## Modify and Adjust

As your children grow and develop, they will reveal parts of themselves to you that will support your planning and enhance your ability to support them. Talk to lots of (nonjudgmental) people so you gain insight into raising this human that may exist through you but is not OF you. Initially refrain from trying to "convince" nay-sayers to see your point of view, and instead direct your energies towards ascertaining your next best option. Maintain in the forefront of your mind that you are here to raise up your children not to please them or be their best friend. Find support and validation in support groups and with your spouse. Proceed with the end goal in mind so you can help your child realize their potential on their own timeline. Learn the rules so you can manipulate them in your favor. And add a bookmark folder to your browser entitled "homeschool considerations" so when something you're doing stops working, you can immediately transition into the next thing.

## When You Cannot Completely Homeschool

Many parents will not be able to devote the time to have someone at home with their child enough to make homeschooling a viable option. In this case, it is important to capitalize on out-of-school time. Breaks, weekends, after school, and summers become very important. During these times, have your child take a couple of online enrichment classes. Make a point to hire a tutor that helps them master and excel in math, even if they don't NEED a tutor to get an A in the class. Create a book list and have the child read from this more appropriate list that celebrates her heritage and honors the history of his/her people. Instead of learning Latin or French, have them learn Arabic or Amharic. Together as a family engage in movie nights that showcase films such as Malcolm X, 42, and Jesse. TV shows such as Dear White People can serve as a spring board for exciting discussion that allow for additional teaching. When you apply a homeschooling mindset, you begin to see the entire world as the classroom and incorporate learning opportunities into every activity your child engages in.

# Chapter 21: What Homeschooling Can Look Like

## A Deeper Exploration of the Various Options

### Using ONLINE School

Online schools typically offer the same courses available to traditional school students. An online school may offer live, teacher-led, interactive online seminars. Students may be able to watch asynchronous video recordings and complete work independently when their schedule allows and then log-on and discuss concepts and ideas in a message board or chatroom fashion with teachers as moderators. And there may be components where credit is awarded for activities that the student already engages in. Online schools are ideal for elite athletes, actors/actresses, performers, or other students who spend the majority of their time working, training, traveling, or auditioning. Further, there are online public schools that offer some of the same benefits. However, public school in any of its iterations (charter, online, traditional) will have additional requirements and limitations imposed, such as required curriculum and standardized testing.

**Examples:** Calvert, Dwight Global, Stanford Online High School. Online public school example: Connections Academy

### Using HYBRID School

Hybrid schools are schools that offer classes and curriculum to homeschool students. The student attends school for two or three days a week and work their syllabi for the remaining days at home. An advantage of hybrid models is they hold parents accountable by moving the student along a course plan throughout the year. Additionally, the entire curriculum is constructed and vetted by professional educators, which removes that task from the parent. The school year of a hybrid school typically resembles that of the local public schools, which might diminish freedom and flexibility for some students. Additionally, while hybrid models allow for parental override and interventions, it is not the parent that constructs or executes the curriculum.

Hybrid models are good for families looking to transition from a traditional setting to a homeschool setting and desire the intermittent "classroom" experience.

A pre-formulated, vetted curriculum is an added plus. Accountability of external evaluators coupled with their expertise helps offload this task from the parent. The price tag on hybrid schools are often a fraction of the cost of a comparable private school, making this choice a top contender for many new-to-homeschooling families.

**Examples:** Gray Matter, Coram Deo Academy, and Regina Caeli Classical Hybrid Education in the Catholic Tradition

### Using BOX Curriculum

Schools such as Oak Meadow and Global Village School offer parents a complete curriculum that is teacher supported, possibly even teacher evaluated, but typically it is the parents executing the curriculum. This execution can also be by way of private tutors, online or in-person. Box curriculum is good for families that have multiple children and want to mind expenditures. Also, a box curriculum allows the parents to have more control over what is presented, how it's presented, and methods of evaluation. Box curriculum is a great choice for parents new to homeschooling and looking to keep costs down while having external, vetted lesson plans available for asynchronous administration.

**Examples:** Kamali Academy, Oak Meadow, Global Village School

### Using ONLINE CLASSES

Over time, a parent may realize that they have the wherewithal to construct a curriculum utilizing individual online class options (combined with other methods). Online classes are great because oftentimes one can find EXCELLENT teachers around the world that can share great ideas and insights with your scholar for a fraction of the price of having them physically in your presence. This is the power of the internet. Online classes range from selecting from a menu of options from a website like Well Trained Mind Academy or Thinkwell, to reaching out to an individual person/professor and simply asking them to work with you child. Online classes are great options for parents and scholars who prefer to tailor the educational experience beyond what can be offered by an entire online school with a pre-fabricated curriculum.

**Examples:** Well Trained Mind Academy, Online G3, Athena Academy, Art of Problem Solving, Elements of Mathematics Foundation

## Using Tutors and Teachers

If you do the math, the price tag a single student pays for elite, selective private school would allow you to essentially hire a part-time private in-home teacher. If you have multiple children, the cost of hiring a certified, private, part-time teacher is LESS THAN the private school tuition. Depending on the difficultly of the subject matter, and the level of advancement, hiring a private tutor/teacher is about $20-40 per hour. If the teacher came to your house for four hours (which is plenty) four days a week to teach two or more students, the cost ranges from about $320/week or $1280/month to twice that. Private preschool tuition in most metroplexes in the United States exceeds $1280/month (for one student). Doing the math, it's not a stretch to realize that hiring your own choice teacher to teach your child exactly at their level is not beyond the realm of possibility for many families. Additionally, if you consider that you may not need to rely on a tutor/teacher for four hours a day four times a week if you utilize other methods of education (such as online, hybrid schools, or box curricula) the price tag on this portion can diminish markedly. Private tutors are good for subjects that are highly specialized (such as music, performance, athletic coaching, speaking coaching, higher-level math, integration of learning differences in various subjects, and supplemental support in areas of difficultly).

## Dual-Enrollment

The hidden gem of homeschooling is dual-enrollment. If the goal for your young scholar entails a college degree, dual-enrollment is worth investigating. Oftentimes, in order to utilize and capitalize on this opportunity, a student only needs to apply to the local community college and select classes that do not demand the prerequisite "test score." Courses such as private music lessons can be selected at the local community college, often for less than $200 for the entire semester, which is great cost savings when compared to the normal and expected cost of community private music lessons.

Additionally, passing the "college-readiness exam" oftentimes is a task that can be accomplished with very short-term preparation of an average middle school student. Once this is passed (likely some variation of the College Board's Accuplacer), the student is eligible to take college core classes. If enough of these classes are taken (both non-core, and core), the student can apply to college/university as a transfer and bypass all the "freshman requirements" such as SAT/ACT, Subject tests, etc. This is a great option for students who are looking to start (and finish) their college careers early, or those who may find early career exploration useful.

## Combination of all the Above

Overtime an experienced homeschool parent realizes that no "prepackaged" curriculum is perfect. If your student can adapt and go with the flow, a change-up may not be warranted. However, many homeschool parents discover that their child is better served if they mix and match the curriculum—selecting some online courses, hiring a part-time tutor, and perhaps participating in a hybrid school until the child is old enough to engage in dual-enrollment at the local community college. Utilization of college credit by exam (CLEP) is helpful. Independent study (or as a punctuation of lessons learned via online classes or via private tutors) can be credentialed with CLEP or AP exams. And homeschool students are privy to both of these opportunities.

## Typical days

### 4th Grade
### At-home day for a student in a hybrid school

9:30 a.m. – Wake up, clean up, and get breakfast

10:00 a.m. – 11:30 a.m. – Do a Singapore Math assignment given by hybrid school teacher. Parents help with questions perhaps by finding additional online videos to watch such as Khan Academy. Breaks for snacks and bathroom are permitted, but supervision is required so they don't become excessive.

11:30 a.m. – 11:45 a.m. – Break

11:45 a.m. – 12:30 p.m. – Language arts work (*Spelling You See* lesson, *Reading Detective* story, *Handwriting Without Tears* lesson)

12:30 p.m. – 1:00 p.m. – Lunch

1:00 p.m. – 1:30 p.m. – Science (MEL Chemistry experiment, or Crash Course Kids videos)

1:30 p.m. – 2:00 p.m. – Spanish (watch children's TV in Spanish or play Spanish Duolingo)

School from 10:00 a.m. – 2:00 p.m. (4 hours with about 3.5 hours of instruction/work time)

Afterschool activities typically start about 5:30 p.m., such as Girl Scouts, Best Brains, choir rehearsal, or soccer practice. Once or twice a week, the day may be extended (or not every subject covered) because of in-home music lessons or enrichment tutoring. If the child needs more time to complete math, perhaps skip handwriting for the day. If a hybrid school is utilized, this would represent an "at-home" day, and the "at-school" day would be a typical 9:00 a.m. – 3:00 p.m. day where you drop the child off at school and pick them up afterwards.

## 7th Grade
## Typical Day for a Student That Takes Online Classes

10:00 a.m. – Wake up, clean up, and get breakfast

10:30 a.m. – 12:30 p.m. – Art of Problem Solving Pre-Algebra daily work

12:30 p.m. – 1:00 p.m. – Independent biology work as taught and assigned by Athena Advanced Academy instructor

1:00 p.m. – 1:50 p.m. – Live, interactive, online Well Trained Mind Fundamentals in Writing class

2:00 p.m. – 2:30 p.m. – Lunch

2:30 p.m. – 3:30 p.m. – Modern U.S. History Through Movies via Online G3

School from 10:30 a.m. – 3:30 p.m. (5 hours with about 4.5 hours of instruction/work time)

Afterschool time can be used for further enrichment or development of hobbies. Additionally, the school day can start earlier and compressed to extend from about 8:00 a.m. – noon to free up the student to spend the rest of the day participating in elite training, special interests, or areas of further desired learning. Finally, the day may be expanded if an in-home music teacher has mid-day lessons, or a math tutor comes to review and help with work "after school" at 5:00 p.m. for a couple of hours a couple times a week.

## 10th Grade
### Using Dual-Enrollment and Online Classes

Dual-enrollment (DE) classes at local community colleges may be scheduled all on the same days. On school days, the schedule will look much like a typical school day with the student on campus for two or three classes with in-between and after-class time spent working on assignments for those classes. DE classes can include core classes such as English composition or U.S. history, or DE classes can allow for career investigation or possible introduction into various study plans, such as geography or computer programming. One semester of DE coursework is credited as an entire year of high school coursework with honors. If a student is taking DE courses, there is no need to add a ton of other at-home coursework to their plate.

At-home days may look something like this:

10:00 a.m. – Wake up, clean up, and get breakfast

10:30 a.m. – 12:30 p.m. – Pre-Calculus using a combination of Khan Academy, Teaching Textbooks, and private tutor support in preparation of taking and passing the Pre-Calculus CLEP

12:30 p.m. – 3:30 p.m. – Work on school work for the dual-enrollment classes (for example an English composition paper and a biology lab report). DE courses may actually require more time than a couple of hours. Hiring a private tutor to help the student with these assignments may be helpful.

Once in high school, the school days will vary from student to student, depending on their interests and extracurriculars. For instance, if the student is looking to enter into a STEM field, such as chemistry, with an ultimate goal of becoming a physician, the DE courses taken (biology, chemistry, physics, calculus) will require many more hours of study than if that same student opts to take a core class such as Art Appreciation or ceramics. Additionally, that student may look for opportunities to shadow community physicians, which may shift the times she is available to engage in the academic coursework, finding herself completing math assignments after dinner. If the student desires to be a video game designer, degree plan requirements may lead him to select a computer programming DE course and spend hours of his "free time" designing games to create a portfolio of work. High school is a time of semi-specialization to inform college selection and degree plan choices.

**Chapter 22: Preparing for College**

## The Examinations of College Prep

It's important to prepare for exams when possible. Even when taking the SCAT, SAT, or ACT for one of the national talent searches, I recommend you invest in some exam prep for your scholar. As a homeschooler, objective data of academic performance will be required of you by most colleges and universities. Examinations make up the bulk of presentable objective data. The Princeton Review offers great online test prep. There are many local, in-person options available in most metroplexes to accommodate students who prefer a classroom setting.

**College entry** – ACT and SAT (familiarization with both will help your child select the best option that will highlight his strengths). Most colleges still require one of these exams for admission consideration. With the exclusion of the highest scorers, these two exams are essentially interchangeable as all four-year colleges and universities accept both exams. However, for the highest scorers, the SAT has added advantage of allowing consideration into the National Merit Scholarship Program via the PSAT. Additionally, the SAT is required for consideration into Johns Hopkins' Center for Talented Youth Study of Exceptional Talent (SET) program.

**CLEP** – College Level Examination Program. CLEP exams are a great way to "legitimize" a homeschool transcript and gather college credit while doing so. The exam is relatively inexpensive, can be taken any time of the year, has great prep books easily obtained online, and can be retaken if not passed without penalty. Many colleges award credit for CLEP passes, particularly for lower-level courses allowing students to "test out" of basic courses if they have the ability to do higher-level work in the subject matter. I highly recommend preparing your child to take the College Algebra CLEP after completing a homeschool algebra 2 program because this is a very doable exam for most students and may even allow the student to meet his entire college math requirement depending on their degree plan.

**Accuplacer** – An exam that was developed by the College Board and is a diagnostic and placement examination for college students. Many college systems use some form of the Accuplacer (re-packaged and re-branded to suit their needs) to determine if a student is "college ready." A college-ready student is permitted to take DE classes that meet college core requirements. Additionally, a student that is deemed to be "college ready" by exam has demonstrated that he or she knows enough high school, and while there are always more things to learn, will likely do well if graduated from homeschool high school for early college entry. Early college entry works well for motivated students who may not be passionate about pursuing any particular career and would like to move on to college to further explore options that are often not available in high school. In Texas, the Accuplacer for college-readiness assessment is called the Texas Success Initiative. Once the student meets college-readiness criteria, they are permitted to enroll in community college.

**Advanced Placement Exams** – AP exams can be taken by homeschoolers at their local high school with public school students. It is possible to self-study for an AP exam, and do well (participation in an AP class is not necessary or required to sit for the AP exams). AP exams demonstrate to colleges that your scholar has objectively mastered the material at a level comparable to other students applying for that same spot. AP exams have a few drawbacks. They are only offered once a year and fitting that into the schedule while dealing with the public school system is a headache. The College Board sends the entire transcript to the colleges and universities, so a low performance may hurt admissions and scholarship offers. The most elite schools do not award college credit for AP exams. For these reasons, CLEP exams and DE classes are better legitimizers of the homeschool academic transcript.

**SAT Subject Tests** – SAT subject tests are subject-specific exams that showcase high-level knowledge in a particular subject. Many elite schools require two or three of these subject area exams of homeschoolers. It is possible to study for both the AP and SAT subject test in a particular subject (study once, test twice).

**Early College/Transfer** – Alternatively, there is a very nice and infrequently used side door into colleges that involves taking DE courses, and then transferring into the university. There are some nuances to this strategy including knowing how the DE credits are documented, knowing the difference between true freshman, super senior, as well as who is considered a "transfer" versus a "freshman," regardless of the number of DE credits completed. Expansion on this strategy is beyond the scope of this book but is an excellent option that deserves to be mentioned.

Considering all of the various examinations required of homeschoolers for entry into elite colleges and universities as a freshman, it's important to plot and plan a path to completion of these various tasks from about seventh grade through eleventh grade (ages 12 or 13 through 16 or 17). Colleges won't see work done in twelfth grade so these tasks need to be completed by the end of JUNIOR year. In order to take the nine plus exams—ACT/SAT twice, PSAT for NMSP, three SAT subject tests, and three AP exams (or CLEP or DE classes)—before college applications open in the August prior to senior year, your scholar will have to start in seventh or eighth grade. Also, if your student wants to further enhance the application with competition Olympiad participation, meaningful research, and/or build a portfolio, a plan of action has to be in place by middle school that incorporates these items as well. Therefore, thinking ahead and planning with the end goal in mind is essential.

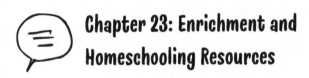

# Chapter 23: Enrichment and Homeschooling Resources

## Math Enrichment

For your child to be a competitive mathlete and a national contender, math enrichment is mandatory. Additionally, good math training builds problem-solving skills that extrapolate into all areas of life.

- Awesome Math Academy
- Art of Problem Solving

Math enrichment includes preparing for the following competitions:

**American Mathematics Competition (AMC) exams 8, 10, 12, and the American Invitational Mathematics Examination (AIME)** – Advanced math training used to be unavailable to most students prior to the internet. Now, there are online programs such as Awesome Math and Art of Problem Solving and Worldwide Online Olympiad Training (WOOT) that are great preparatory programs. This level of math training is simply not available at local high schools. Doing well on these exams, particularly the AIME, will enhance applications to elite universities. Additionally, if your student desires to study a subject heavy in math enrichment is critical otherwise she will be at a disadvantage in rigorous programs that attract the best global students because our American high schools do not teach the level (and type) of math necessary to compete. Competition math training begins to level the playing-field.

https://www.maa.org/

**USAMTS (USA Math Talent Search)** – Students have an entire month to answer five questions. They upload their answers. As with the AMC 10 and AMC 12, those students who score well enough on the USAMTS are invited to sit for the AIME. Top scorers on the AIME are then invited to sit for the USA Mathematical Olympiad (USAMO). These students represent the top math students in the country and are rewarded with scholarships and admissions into the most exclusive and elite colleges and universities. The top USAMO students are selected to attend the Mathematical Olympiad Summer Program, and it is from this group that the U.S. Olympic math team is comprised.

http://www.usamts.org/

**MathCounts** – Homeschool students participating in MathCounts have the advantage of going to the local chapter competition automatically. Most students are competing within their school/districts with internal exams to ascertain who will represent the school and make the representing team.

https://www.mathcounts.org/

**MOEMS (Math Olympiad for Elementary and Middle School)** – This competition allows homeschoolers to enter as a team. There are some stipulations and a fee ($99). The exam is administered by a PICO (Person in Charge of Olympiads) in the home. It is open to other local homschoolers.

**Purple Comet! Math Meet** – Free, online, math team for middle and high schoolers.

https://purplecomet.org/

**Math Kangaroo** – This is an international math competition from grades one through 12 held in March of each year.

http://mathkangaroo.us/

## Academic Competitions

- Physics Olympiad
- Chemistry Olympiad
- Biology Olympiad
- USA Computing Olympiad
- National Science Fairs (such as Siemans Foundation, Google, Intel ISEF, etc.)

## Extracurricular Activity Ideas That Support Healthy Socialization

- Summer interest-based camps (such as Girl Scout camp or space camp)
- Summer academic enrichment camps (such as Duke-Tip, JHU-CTY, PROMYS, THINK Institute)

- Summer camps for special skill development (such as Interlochen or Concordia Language Villages)
- Youth ambassador for a cause
- Group-style academic enrichment (such as Best Brains)
- Chess club or game days
- Math club/Math Circles
- Cotillion
- Sorority/fraternity youth affiliate groups
- 4H
- Scouts
- Poetry slams/spoken word
- Music lessons
- Orchestras
- Bands
- Sports
- Bees (spelling bee, geography bee)
- Archery
- Shooting at a gun range
- Astronomy club
- Planetarium
- Video game tournaments
- Church
- Choir
- Recreation center sports
- Martial arts
- Robotics and Lego club
- Speech and debate
- Career exposure opportunities such as shadowing a physician, veterinarian, lawyer, etc. for networking, documentation of shadowing hours, firsthand learning about

various professional fields, meeting potential mentors, and exposure to pipeline programs.

- Mom groups offer local connection with national reach for women who mother Black children and offer great opportunities for positive, supervised socialization, such as Jack and Jill of America, Incorporated and Mocha Moms, Incorporated.

### Field-trip Ideas

- Trips with parents/family to anywhere
- Physics & engineering festivals
- Botanical gardens/nature centers
- Escape rooms
- Ifly indoor skydiving
- Tastebuds Kitchen
- Zoo
- Aquariums
- Library (many public libraries have great programming geared towards youth, and some specifically target homeschoolers)
- Pumpkin patch
- Community vegetable garden
- Farmers market
- Humane society
- Book store/story time
- Puppet shows
- Bee-keeper hive
- Local parks
- Recreation centers

## Online Schools

### Oak Meadow

https://www.oakmeadow.com/

Founded in 1975, and a Waldorf-inspired curriculum, Oak Meadow provides a flexible, progressive education for independent learning from kindergarten to twelfth grade.

### Global Village School

https://www.globalvillageschool.org/

GVS is an accredited international distance learning school. Their values include peace, compassion, justice, sustainability, community, integrity, and appreciation of diversity, caring for the Earth and our fellow beings, creativity, and living an authentic and meaningful life.

### Kamali Academy

http://www.kamaliacademy.com/

Pre-K through eighth grade online curriculum is serving thousands. It's Afrikan-centered and flexible.

### Well Trained Mind Academy

http://www.wtmacademy.com/

Their goal is to bring the time-tested benefits of Classical Education within the reach of every family. They choose to partner with parents, not replace them, by supplementing their existing home curriculum with experienced instructors in a clearly classical approach to each subject.

## Shmoop

https://www.shmoop.com/

WE SPEAK STUDENT®
Your one-stop shop for everything academic.

## Enki Education

http://www.enkieducation.org/index.htm

Enki Education offers a unique and innovate way to approach living and learning.

## Calvert Education

http://www.calverteducation.com/homeschool

Provides a proven and time-tested curriculum, with all the tools and support necessary to ensure you are the best teacher your child has ever had.

## Live Education!

https://www.live-education.com/introducing-live-education/

Produces homeschooling supplies for families inspired by the Waldorf perspective. They offer individualized curriculum and pedagogical support (K-8) to form the basis for full-time home education or to supplement traditional schooling.

### Time4Learning

https://www.time4learning.com/secular/index.shtml

Each of the secular activities in the Time4Learning curriculum is standards-based and correlates with the average public school curriculum. That means that each one of our lessons (even the science and social studies!) is free of religious undertones or biases. Exercises are presented via animated, interactive, multimedia lessons that feel more like video games than learning exercises. Kids genuinely enjoy the funny sound effects and the quirky cartoon characters delivering the lessons. Plus, the student-paced nature of the program gives them a feeling of independence and sense of ownership over their progress, which is a great motivator.

### Acellus Academy

https://www.acellusacademy.com/

Accredited online school for grades K-12. Provides a rigorous academic experience that is individualized and tailored to each student's unique learning needs.

### Stanford Online High School

https://onlinehighschool.stanford.edu/

Offering courses for grades 7–12, Stanford Online High School is a highly selective independent school, where dedicated instructors help talented students worldwide pursue their passions in real-time, online seminars.

### Dwight Global Online School

https://www.dwight.edu/dwight-global-online-school

An online school like no other, Dwight Global combines real-time online video conferencing seminars, Oxford-style tutorials, and a college-style schedule to provide students with the intimacy of an independent school coupled with the freedom to pursue their passions.

### Online G3

https://www.onlineg3.com/

Online G3 nurtures critical and creative thinking in a diverse community of gifted learners by providing a supportive and flexible online learning environment. By pairing passionate teachers with engaging and interactive academic content, G3 offers appropriate acceleration within an accredited, secular, and affordable education program.

### Athena Academy

https://athenasacademy.com/

Their mission is to create a stimulating and engaging educational environment that challenges gifted and talented students and promotes learning in a positive and rewarding atmosphere. They design captivating courses that can be tailored to meet the goals in each student's educational plan, including homeschoolers and those looking for enrichment.

## Great Courses Plus

https://www.thegreatcoursesplus.com/education

The Great Courses Plus provides you with a cost-effective way to optimize your curriculum experience. You'll get uninterrupted access to hundreds of courses taught by the world's greatest professors.

## Homeschool Courses

### Homeschool Math

https://www.homeschoolmath.net/

HomeschoolMath.net is a comprehensive math resource site for homeschooling parents, parents, and teachers that includes free math worksheets, lessons, online math games, lists, ebooks, a curriculum guide, reviews, and more. The resources emphasize understanding of concepts instead of mechanical memorization of rules.

## IXL

https://www.ixl.com/

IXL is an immersive K-12 learning experience that provides comprehensive, standards-aligned content for math, language arts, science, and social studies.

### Liberty's Kids

https://www.youtube.com/channel/UC5pJi9mLIy38m2e_u3sboKQ/featured

Two teenage reporters cover the events of the Revolutionary War for Ben Franklin's newspaper, The Philadelphia Gazette.

### Amoeba Sisters

https://www.youtube.com/user/AmoebaSisters

Two sisters on a mission to demystify science with humor and relevance by creating videos, GIFs, comics, and resources (such as their handouts and Unlectured Series). They love to empower teacher and student creators.

### Bozeman Science

http://www.bozemanscience.com/biology-main-page/

Paul Andersen is an educational consultant and YouTube creator living in Bozeman, MT. Paul is an experienced educator having taught science in Montana for 20 years. Paul was the 2011 Montana Teacher of the Year and was also one of four finalists for the 2011 National Teacher of the Year. In addition to teaching, Paul has created hundreds of YouTube science tutorials that have been viewed millions of times by students around the world. In

2012, Paul was selected by YouTube as one of ten YouTube Edu Gurus.

## Thinkwell

https://www.thinkwell.com/

Thinkwell creates dynamic, video-based learning materials for core curriculum subject areas. They aim to facilitate transformative learning experiences inside and outside the classroom by giving educators and students the tools, technology, and content they need to succeed. They view education as an opportunity to inspire curiosity and strive to create a generation of critical thinkers who solve problems with confidence. In all areas, they champion the spirit of learning by thinking well.

## TedEd

https://ed.ted.com/

Lessons worth sharing. Use engaging videos on TED-Ed to create customized lessons.

## PBS Space Time

https://www.youtube.com/channel/UC7_gcso9iThXybpVgjHZ_7g

Space Time explores the outer reaches of space, the craziness of astrophysics, the possibilities of sci-fi, and anything else you can think of beyond Planet Earth with our astrophysicist host: Matthew O'Dowd.

## edX

www.edx.org

Founded by Harvard University and MIT in 2012, edX is an online learning destination and MOOC provider, offering high-quality courses from the world's best universities and institutions to learners everywhere.

## Crash Course

https://thecrashcourse.com/

At Crash Course, they believe that high-quality educational videos should be available to everyone for free. The Crash Course team has produced more than 15 courses to date, and these videos accompany high school—and college-level classes ranging from the humanities to the sciences. Crash Course transforms the traditional textbook model by presenting information in a fast-paced format, enhancing the learning experience.

## Udemy

https://www.udemy.com/

Udemy is a global marketplace for learning and teaching online where students are mastering new skills and achieving their goals by learning from an extensive library of over 80,000 courses taught by expert instructors.

## Coursera

https://www.coursera.org/

Coursera provides universal access to the world's best education, partnering with top universities and organizations to offer courses online.

## Universal Class

https://www.universalclass.com/index.htm

They provide high-quality online courses to help you learn the skills needed to achieve your goals. The courses are not just tutorials, they are real. They include lessons, exams, assignments, discussion boards and an instructor to help you master the learning outcomes.

## ALEKS

https://www.aleks.com/

Assessment and Learning in Knowledge Spaces is a web-based, artificially intelligent assessment and learning system. ALEKS uses adaptive questioning to quickly and accurately determine exactly what a student knows and doesn't know in a course. ALEKS then instructs the student on the topics she/he is most ready to learn. As a student works through a course, ALEKS periodically reassesses the student to ensure that topics learned are also retained. ALEKS courses are very complete in their topic coverage and ALEKS avoids multiple-choice questions. A student who shows a high level of mastery of an ALEKS course will be successful in the actual course she/he is taking.

## Hybrid Schools

### Gray Matter

http://www.graymatterdfw.com/

Gray Matter is a brick-and-mortar school offering classes for homeschooled, middle and high school students. Students are placed into classes based on ability, not age, so your student can achieve as much as they want.

Classes generally meet twice a week. You can take one or as many courses necessary to meet your student's needs. Customize your education!

### Regina Caeli Classical Hybrid Education in the Catholic Tradition

http://www.rcahybrid.org/Default

Regina Caeli is a private, independent university model hybrid education center (combining homeschooling 3 days a week with a structured two day a week academy) operating in the Catholic tradition.

### University Model Schools International (UMSI)

http://umsi.org/

Christian-based organization offering certification to private hybrid schools that meet certain requirements.

It's important to note that many schools offer a hybrid type of learning but have decided to not jump through the hoops to become "certified" as a trademarked "university-model" school. The certification is not important and parents should not let the school's participation (or non-participation) in this organization be a deciding factor in choice selection. Actually, the best hybrid schools that offer a more diverse and flexible educational curriculum will likely NOT hold this certification. However, I list it here to serve as a reference.

## Tutoring

### It's Not Complicated Tutoring

http://www.inctutoring.com/

### Care.com

https://www.care.com/

### Frog Tutoring

https://frogtutoring.com/

## Local Universities and Community Colleges

Reaching out to local university and community colleges to find students who can tutor.

## Our Favorite Books and Workbooks

## Homeschool and Parenting

- *What High Schools Don't Tell You (And Other Parents Don't Want You to Know)* by Elizabeth Wissner-Gross
- *Siblings Without Rivalry* by Adele Faber and Elaine Mazlish
- *The Battle Hymn of the Tiger Mother* by Amy Chua
- *The Mis-Education of the Negro* by Carter G. Woodson
- *Reading Reflex* by Carmen McGuiness and Geoffrey McGuiness
  Helps adults teach children to be better readers
- *College Planning Using Dual-Enrollment* by Kathe Lee
- *A Parent's Guide to Gifted Children* by James T. Webb
- *Mindset* by Carol S. Dweck
- *Conversations with God for Parents* by Neale Donald Walsch
- *The Conscious Parent* by Shefali Tsabary

## Language Arts

- Phonics
- Explode the Code
- ABC Mouse

- Nabi Tablet reading games

## English Grammar

- Kamali Academy *Afrikan-Centered Grammar Workbook for Middle Grades* by Samori Camara
- *First Language Lessons*
- Institute for Excellence in Writing
- Michael Clay Thompson Grammar Program

## Spelling

- *Spelling You See*
- *A Reason for Spelling*

## Writing

- The Complete Writer Series
- Institute for Excellence in Writing
- *Sentence Composing for Middle School* by Don Killgallon
- *Paragraphs for Middle School* by Don and Jenny Killgallon
- Brave Writer

## Reading Comprehension

- *Reading Detective* Series
- SAT Barron's Picture That SAT Words in a Flash

## Handwriting

- *A Reason for Handwriting*

- *Handwriting without Tears*
- Kamali Academy Handwriting

## Math

- Teaching Textbooks
- Art of Problem Solving & Beast Academy
- Elements of Mathematics Foundation
- Holt Series
- Math Mammoth
- *String Straight-Edge and Shadow: The Story of Geometry* by Julia E. Diggins
- *The Adventures of Penrose the Mathematical Cat* by Theoni Pappas
- ALEKS

## Social Science

- Kamali Academy
  - *Classical Africa* by Molefi Kete Asante
  - *African American History A Journey of Liberation* by Molefi Kete Asante
  - *Countering the Conspiracy to Destroy Black Boys* by Jawanza Kunjufu
  - *Creation Myths of the World* by David Adams Lemming
  - Evan-Moor Africa
  - *Nile Valley Contributions to Civilization* by Anthony T. Browder
- *Story of the World* series
- Liberty's Kids on YouTube

- *A History of the U.S.: Ten-Volume Set* by Joy Hakim

## Science

- Amoeba Sisters
- Khan Academy
- Thinkwell
- Crash Courses
- *Life of Fred* series
- MEL Science
- Quizlet
- PBS Kids
- PBS Space Time

## Various Subjects

- Great Courses Plus
- Time4Learning
- Acellus Academy – powerhomeschool.com
- Ted-ed

## Parent Support Groups

## On Facebook

- Village Moms
- Brilliant in Color
- Secular Homeschoolers
- Decolonize Homeschool
- African American Homeschool Moms

- Black Homeschool Families
- African American Homeschool Holistic Living
- The Black Homeschool Connection
- Homeschooling Highschool to College
- Paying for College 101
- Secular Homeschool Families
- Rock Your Homeschool
- Parenting During a Trump Presidency
- MS & HS: for Secular Eclectic Academic Homeschoolers
- College Credit by Exam Homeschool
- Homeschool Resource Exchange
- Gifted Unschoooling
- Homeschoool Math Dad
- Raising Poppies
- The Relaxed Homeschool Community
- Secular Families Who Homeschool
- Homeschooling Around the World
- Secular Homeschool Curriculum
- Homeschool Planning & Organizing
- Worldschoolers People of Color
- Homeschooling Mensans
- Homeschool Freethinkers
- Well Trained Mind
- Homeschooling with The Great Courses
- Homeschooling for College Credit
- Plus many local subgroups of the above or unique groups that are area- or interest-specific.

## On Yahoo!

- Homeschool to college: hs2coll

- Homeschooling Mensans
- Secular_homeschools
- HorizonHS

## Forums

- College Confidential
- Well Trained Mind Forums
- Mothering Forums (mothering.com)

## Gifted Advocacy

- Davidson Institute
- Texas Parents of the Profoundly Gifted
- PG Retreat
- National Association for Gifted Children
- American Mensa
- SENG – Support the Emotional Needs of the Gifted
- Texas Association for the Gifted & Talented

## Homeschool Advocacy

Homeschool Legal Defense Association (HSLDA)

**Chapter 24: General Homeschooling Advice**

1. Join supportive homeschool parenting groups and discuss issues there. Don't expect your friends and family to understand or support your decision. Therefore, don't share details with nay-sayers.
2. Learn your children. If possible, take them to get evaluated by a psychologist so you can ascertain their learning style and areas of giftedness. Learn their personality characteristics. Spend time with them, talking to them, and asking them questions about their hopes, dreams, thoughts, and plans. Allow them to participate in the process.
3. Set your goals. Realistically try to ascertain what type of educational path would best suit your child. Not every child should be forced into a tech school or an elite private school. Their educational and career goals may be better served at an art school or local public school. Disregard name brand and societal expectations, and do an honest assessment, and calculate the expected return on investment of pursuing various paths. Do not simply try to replicate the public school.
4. Start with a program that is simple. A pre-planned curriculum, a hybrid school, a box curriculum, or an online school.
5. Be prepared for constant adjustments and changes, often

occurring mid-year such as switching programs or text-books, dropping or adding subjects, and modifying grade levels.

6. Realize your child needs to be able to formulate thoughts, solve problems, and communicate thoughts and solutions to other humans. Decide what he/she needs to learn in order to do this. Therefore, not all the classic subjects need to be incorporated into your homeschool. Instead of Greek mythology, perhaps Ethiopian history. Instead of Latin, perhaps Amharic. Instead of British literature, per-haps African proverbs would be more empowering and mean more to the Black student. I've found that essential subjects include math and language arts. I also incorpo-rate opportunities for exposure to the arts, science, health, and spirituality.

7. Sleeping in is great. It helps maintain health, helps with learning retention, helps with personality development, and improves family dynamics. Being tired zaps people of their ability to present the best and brightest version of themselves to the world.

8. Realize that not every day has to include every subject; and further, it is okay to put some subjects on the back burner for a week or more and focus on a particularly in-teresting or difficult topic instead.

9. Hire help. Babysitters, tutors, coaches, music teachers, and other necessary professionals. Remember, you are an educational coordinator, administrating and facilitating the educational experience of your children. You are not necessarily the schoolteacher. You can outsource the parts that someone else can do better.

10. Your time with your children is the most valuable gift you

can provide. As they approach tween/teen years, your presence becomes even more necessary as they formulate their very sense of themselves and their positions in the world. While the care of a baby can be outsourced, that of a tween/teen will have a huge missing element if not done by a parental figure. You want their inner voice to be one that is guided by you. That can only happen if you are present and they hear you talk in real-time about life-issues that present in their lives. In order to become a wise way-shower for your children, they have to respect you as a trustworthy guide. That cannot be done if the bulk of their time is immersed in the chaos of damaging environments, and the only time left to undo the damage is at the end of each day when everyone is running on empty and not the best versions of themselves.

## Haley's Note

Being in a classroom where you have to wait on everybody to catch up all the time is like constantly pausing a movie that you're very interested in so others can "discuss" and "understand" it before YOU are able to continue watching the movie. You want to yell, "I don't NEED or want to discuss the movie; can we just stop talking and press play and keep watching it?!"

Or it's like a VERY SLOW internet connection. You know what you want to do, your brain is going a mile a minute with excitement to learn something new or research something on Google, but the internet just spins and spins...and you must wait! You just want to THROW the phone.

Being in a classroom where you constantly must wait and slow down is like being stuck in traffic all the time. You cannot move until everybody else does. And even then, you can't move further than they do. It's horrible. It literally gives me a headache.

**Chapter 25: Frequently Asked Questions**

### Why did you start homeschooling?

I started homeschooling as my oldest was finishing up fifth grade. The main impetus for making the switch was my discomfort with gradual, subtle changes I observed in her personality. She began to diminish her life light because her fire made schoolmates, and the educational establishment, uncomfortable. She gradually started embracing disempowering mindsets and gender roles. Additionally, I felt the academic rigor was lacking as no student could be left behind. By necessity, the teachers had to teach to the bottom half of students. Year after year, Haley wasn't learning anything significantly new or interesting. And the overemphasis on the standardized testing removed creativity and tailoring from the classroom.

### What curriculum do you recommend?

Curriculum is highly personal and should be tailored to the individual child and family based on long- and short-term goals, career aspirations, and desired university experiences. Financial resources, necessary parental oversight, age of the child, and local opportunities are also key factors in helping to determine the best curriculum. In general, I recommend starting with a more comprehensive curriculum, such as Oak Meadow, or box curriculum, because there is an element of comfort and confidence that allows a new homeschooling parent to feel prepared and get their bearing while they transition.

Also, incorporation of an online platform is fantastic. Deciding which areas are important to you and your child for them to be knowledgeable enough to reach their career and life goals will help with focus. Well Trained Mind Academy offers a plethora of a la carte options. The Art of Problem Solving challenges young students in areas of math and critical thinking. Elements of Mathematics Foundation offers an innovative problem-solving platform. Teaching Textbooks provides lectures and problems in a light, fun, aesthetically pleasing manner. And there are also online high schools, such as Dwight Online High School where "Grownish" star Yara Shahidi graduated from, or Stanford Online High School, which consistently ranks among America's top high schools.

Additionally, it is important to ascertain the ultimate end goal of this part of the student's educational journey. A great book that helps offer some perspective is *What High Schools Don't Tell You (And Other Parents Don't Want You to Know)* by Elizabeth Wissner-Gross. Through reading this, it's possible to see how much planning and research goes into helping your children realize their greatest potential.

### How did you make your children stand out?

It's important for college admission and beyond for your child to have and develop unique attributes. It is a mistake to push kids into activities just because they are popular with no regard to their natural talents, skills, interests, and without consideration for how the return on the investment will prove worthwhile. For most children, choosing football, soccer, or basketball is a total waste of time and resources. If the goal is recreation, exercise, friendship, sportsmanship, and fun, these overpopulated activities may fit the bill perfectly. However, if the goal is investment in something that will allow your child to stand out in a crowd, selecting a less popular activity (sport or instrument) will allow them to shine and take top spots. If it's all the same to you and your child, why not choose something they can dominate with less effort?

### How did you get your child ready for college so young?

For the record, I believe most children can go to college as a young teen. I took Haley from a mediocre fifth grade 10-year-old to an exceptional college freshman at age 13 just by paying attention, advancing her in math, helping ensure she had the proper study techniques and time-management skills, and making her interesting to colleges. Homeschool is interesting. Playing the harp, fencing, and debate are all exceedingly more interesting than public school, soccer, and violin. Interesting and unique activities add value to college essays, interviews, and life stories.

I also allowed my child to progress at her own pace, enhancing areas of skill and remediating areas of weakness. I focused on enrichment that played to her strengths because it is by focusing on gifts and strengths that people are able to contribute their gifts to humanity.

### Can parents that work still homeschool?

I think that a ton of homeschooling can take place even if the child attends public school. The mindset of a parent that homeschools is one that does not expect for the public school to provide all that is needed for the child to thrive. Homeschooling parents consider themselves educational coordinators or facilitators. Even if they need public school to provide daycare so they can work, it is possible (and necessary) for them to still coordinate and facilitate the educational curriculum and experience of their children. Public (or private) school is just one tool in the arsenal to help them do this.

Working parents can homeschool if they realize that schooling can take place at atypical times. Weekends, holidays, breaks, and evenings become prime "schooling" time. Working parents will need to capitalize on the hours they have with their child. Additionally, the coordination and facilitation of the homeschool plan can be done by the working parent, and the execution of said plan can be outsourced to other family members or hired help. The emphasis I'd like to make is on the coordination and facilitation of the educational plan by the homeschooling parent is what's essential. A parent that has the time and capacity to administrate and coordinate the homeschool plan, and the resources to execute the plan, can homeschool.

### Why can't we expect public school to maximize our children's potential?

Schools are not designed to maximize our individual child's potential. School is designed to educate the masses to "fit into" the workforce. Our school system was designed at a time where the workforce consisted of factories that needed cogs in the wheel. Many aspects of education cannot be confined to a classroom for 40 hours per week nor separated from the rest of life. Additionally, school cannot teach a child who they are. A stranger (that changes each year) cannot take the time (because it takes years) to get to know your child and provide him/her the nuanced components of lessons that only she/he may benefit from.

Schools cannot parent. And teachers cannot replace parents. Raising a child (which includes educating them) is a 24/7 endeavor that cannot be delegated/outsourced in its entirety to an entity designed to take care of the masses because what's good for a population is not necessarily what's going to be good for an individual within said population.

Teachers and traditional schools are only one small part of education. And until parents really embrace this fact and take control of the upbringing of their children, they are going to unsuccessfully look for someone else to take on that role.

**I see some homeschooling parents that are doing a very bad job. Shouldn't our focus be on more regulation for homeschoolers?**

I think we need to ensure policy is enacted based on data. How many kids per 1000 homeschooled kids do poorly? And what is poorly? How many kids per 1000 in public school do poorly? Creating a bureaucracy to provide oversight of homeschool students would cost money. The return on the investment for society would be minimal since a very small relative number of students are homeschooled. That money would be better spent meeting the needs of the larger population of students who use our public school system. Society cannot effectively focus on the individual over the masses and maintain order.

To that end, our legislative focus is on helping the most people. This would entail putting our limited resources into programming that will best serve the most children. After achieving this goal—which would include true integration and diversity, diminishing racial implicit biases of our school leadership and teachers, changing stereotypes, equitable distribution of educational resources, etc.—then we can tackle making it work for outliers.

In the meantime, penalizing parents that seek alternative forms of education will only hurt all students who aren't fitting into the current system. We should care because a large number of children who don't fit are brown, Black, and/or female. Therefore, any new rules will disproportionally prevent the neediest children from having alternatives outside of a system that was not designed with them in mind and are failing them.

### Should we dismantle public school?

A strong and effective public school system is important. Not just for parents who cannot homeschool but for a society. However, there are two conversations people tend to have:

1. What is best for the population?
2. What is best for their individual child and circumstance?

What's best for society is a strong public school system. What's best for your child may be to not participate in that system.

But the system is nonetheless necessary and important. But knowing about (and having access to) other options/choices, I believe, is quintessentially American. Being able to allow for accommodation of a diverse, heterogeneous population is essential.

### Question for Haley: Do you ever think about what you've missed taking this homeschool, radically accelerated pathway to, and through, high school and college?

I am keenly aware of the fact that oftentimes once we select one option, all other options disappear. If I would have stayed on the traditional path, I can only guess what my life would have been like. But I do not see how it could have been better than the path I chose. I do not feel I missed anything that matters. I am not at all interested in attending awkward dances with teenage boys. I am not at all feeling left out of some sister circle of mean girls. I am glad to have avoided mixing racism and defending my right to exist in the midst of trying to learn algebra. I'm honestly not sure what I actually should feel I missed out on.

I went to debutante balls and formal galas. I played team sports and did group work. I have great friends, and we go to the mall and the movies. I have a full social life, active personal life, and excellent academic life. What did I miss out on?

Better perspective is to appreciate and focus on what I've gained by not having to expend energy on the basic elements of navigating this huge, impersonal institution as a Black girl. I was free to focus and excel. My innate and inherent value was celebrated and nurtured in every environment that was charged with educating me. While there's no escaping nay-sayers and mean people who hate anyone that's different—especially during these times—it is not these situations that stick to me and inform my worldview. On the contrary, it is the strong foundation of self-love, self-respect, self-awareness, and positive sense of who I am that gives my feathers their waxy coat, allowing all of the world's negativity to roll right off my back.

# Appendix: American Black History Timeline

*"Of the 12.5 million Africans shipped to the New World during the Transatlantic Slave Trade, fewer than 388,000 arrived in the United States."* – PBS 10 Little Known Black History Facts

## A Timeline

- African Slave Trade – In 1526, the Portuguese completed their first transatlantic voyage to Brazil. For over 400 years, African people were exploited by colonizers so they could manipulate and steal land and resources from indigenous people.
- 1619 – Enslaved Africans imported to Jamestown, Virginia, which was a British Colony.
- Mid-1600s – Africans imported to the Colonies were demoted from indentured servants to slaves without rights, and their children considered property of the slave owner.
- 1600–1800s (over 200 years) Transatlantic Slave Trade (The Middle Passage) – Millions of Africans were shipped to the Americas. The journey took up to six months depending on weather. During that time, African women were raped repeatedly, and the transport conditions were unimaginably horrific. Fifty percent of Africans died prior to the transport, and an additional 20% died during the voyage. Africans were regularly beat to prevent rebellion, and some were sacrificed in a show of force to maintain control over the people (that were considered "cargo") as they out-numbered the crew.

- 1775–1783 – American Revolution. The Thirteen Colonies won independence from Great Britain.
- April 12, 1861 – American Civil War began.
- January 1, 1863 – President Lincoln signed The Emancipation Proclamation, which changed the legal status of 3.1 million slaves in the Confederacy to free. However, the slave had to escape the South to realize freedom.
- May/June 1865 – American Civil War ended. The Union Army controlled all the Confederacy and all slaves were liberated.
- Juneteenth – June 19, 1865. Emancipation of the last remaining enslaved persons in the United States.
- December 18, 1865 – Slavery officially ended with the ratification of the 13th Amendment.
- 1526–1865 – Slavery of people of African descent in America persists (340 years of active and legal slavery).
- 1865–1877 – Rebuilding of the South with full enforcement of the 13th Amendment called Reconstruction with federal troops stationed in the South to enforce the laws of the land and prevent re-enslavement of Blacks.
- Civil Rights Act of 1866 make Blacks full U.S. citizens and repealed the Dred Scott decision.
- 1868 – 14th Amendment granted full U.S. citizenship to American Blacks.
- March 30, 1870 – The 15th Amendment of the U.S. Constitution ratified, giving all male citizens the right to vote (including Black males).
- 1877 – Reconstruction ends on March 31, 1877. The federal troops left, which led to the Gilded Age, where Blacks were on their own with no protections or advocates. This

led to slavery-adjacent practices (such as peonage, share-cropping, and convict leasing) well into the 1900s.

- Since convicts were the de facto new slaves, it was very common for Black men to be arrested and subsequently convicted of false crimes. This is how they created the necessary labor.
- Jim Crow Segregation 1896 – Separate but unequal and no judicial protection.
- World War I – July 28, 1914 – November 11, 1918 – Blacks were needed in Northern factories. European migration was diminished.
- April 1917 – United States entered WWI against Germany primarily because the Germans were preventing American trade with Great Britain and in so doing, sunk American ships. Additionally, Germany kept killing innocent people and sinking unarmed ships, so world opinion turned against Germany.
- 1914–1920 – Great Migration I where 500,000+ Black southerners headed North. One of the largest internal movements of people in American history.
- September 1, 1939–September 2, 1945 – World War II. Hitler and the Nazis invade Poland and France and the United Kingdom declare war. The Allies (United Nations, Soviet Union, United Kingdom, and the United States) vs the Axis (Germany, Japan, Italy). United States enter the war on December 7, 1941 after Japan's attack on Pearl Harbor.
- December 1941 – President Franklin Delano Roosevelt abolished convict leasing.
- 1941-1970 – Great Migration II, where more than five million Blacks with more skill or education moved from the

south to the west, to Los Angeles and Oakland, California, and to the north and Midwest.

# References, Works-Cited, and Additional Reading

## Part 1

### Historical Perspective: Being A Black American

[1]  DeGruy, Joy. "Post Traumatic Slave Syndrome" *America's Legacy of Enduring Injury and Healing, Revised Edition*. Joy Degruy Publications Inc, 2017.

[2]  Carpenter, Zoe. "What's Killing America's Black Infants? Racism is Fueling a National Health Crisis." *The Nation*, 6 March 2017, https://www.thenation.com/article/whats-killing-americas-Black-infants/

[3]  The World Bank Data. "Mortality Rate, infant (Per 1000 Live Births) 1960-2017," 2017 (date accessed 10/7/2018), https://data.worldbank.org/indicator/SP.DYN.IMRT.IN

[4]  Society for the Study of Reproduction. "Developing Countries." 2018 (date accessed 10/7/2018) http://www.ssr.org/DevelopingCountries

[5]  Semprini, Jason. "Black Births Matter: Institution Racism and Infant Mortality Rates in the United States." *Chicago Policy Review*, 2 Mar. 2018, http://chicagopolicyreview.org/2018/03/02/Black-births-matter-institutional-racism-and-infant-mortality-rates-in-the-united-states/

[6]  Lyubansky, Mikhail. "The Health Outcomes of a Racist Society." *Psychology Today*, 7 June 2013.


Dias, Brian G. and Kerry J. Ressler. "Parental Olfactory Experience Influences Behavior and Neural Structure in Subsequent Generations." *Nature Neuroscience*, Jan. 2014, vol. 17, no. 1.

Meserett, Kentake "The Horrors of the Middle Passage." *Kentake Page*, 23 Aug. 2015, http://kentakepage.com/the-horrors-of-the-middle-passage/

Gillespie, Katherine. "Can We Access the Memories of Our Ancestors Through Our DNA?" *Vice*, 20 Dec 2016, https://www.vice.com/en_au/article/ypv58j/genetic-memory

Yehuda, Rachel, et al. "Holocaust Exposure Induced Intergenerational Effects on FKBP5 Methylation." *Biological Psychiatry*, 1 Sept., 2016, vol. 80, no. 5, pp. 372-380.

Klosin, Adam, et al. "Impaired DNA Replication Depresses Chromatin and

Generates a Transgenerationally Inherited Epigenetic Memory." *Science Advances*, 16 Aug. 2017, vol 3, no. 8.

International Slavery Museum. "Life on Board Slave Ships," http://www.liverpoolmuseums.org.uk/ism/slavery/middle_passage/

Mintz, Steven. "The Middle Passage." *Digital History*, 2016 (date accessed 10/7/2018), http://www.digitalhistory.uh.edu/disp_textbook.cfm?smtid=2&psid=446

Robinson, Nathan J. "A Quick Reminder of Why Colonialism Was Bad." *Current Affairs*, 14 Sept. 2017. https://www.currentaffairs.org/2017/09/a-quick-reminder-of-why-colonialism-was-bad

Meltzer, David J. *First Peoples in a New World: Colonizing Ice Age America.* University of California Press, 2009. p. 162.

Fagundes, Nelson J.R., et al. "Mitochondrial Population Genomics Supports a Single Pre-Clovis Origin with a Coastal Route for the Peopling of the Americas." *American Journal of Human Genetics*, 3 March 2008.

Arnesen, Eric, ed. *Black Protest and the Great Migration: A Brief History with Documents.* Bedford/St. Martin's, 2003.

Barbeau, Arthur E. and Florette Henri. *The Unknown Soldiers: African-American Troops in World War I.* Da Capo Press, 1996.

Brown, Nikki. *Private Politics And Public Voices: Black Women's Activism from World War I to the New Deal.* Indiana University Press, 2007.

Ellis, Mark. *Race, War and Surveillance Race, War, and Surveillance: African Americans and the United States Government during World War I.* Indiana University Press, 2001.

Grossman, James R. *Land of Hope: Chicago, Black Southerners, and the Great Migration.* University of Chicago Press, 1989.

Gregory, James N. *The Southern Diaspora: How the Great Migrations of Black and White Southerners Transformed America.* University of North Carolina Press, 2005.

## Being a Child

Robinson, Jennie. "The First Hunter-Gatherers." *The Oxford Handbook of the Archaeology and Anthropology of Hunter-Gatherers*, Apr. 2014, doi: 10.1093/oxfordhb/9780199551224.013.02

Smithsonian National Museum of Nature History. "What Does it Mean to Be Human?" http://humanorigins.si.edu/

History.com. "Hunter Gatherers." *A+E Networks*, 12 May 2018, https://www.history.com/topics/hunter-gatherers

## Being a Black Child in America

[1] Children's Defense Fund. "Child Poverty in America 2016: National Analysis." 18 Sept. 2017, http://www.childrensdefense.org/library/data/child-poverty-in-america-2016.pdf

[2] Ratcliffe, Caroline. "Child Poverty and Adult Success." *Urban Institute*, Sept. 2015.

[3] "Effects of Poverty, Hunger and Homelessness on Children and Youth." *American Psychological Association*, http://www.apa.org/pi/families/poverty.aspx/

[4] Kornbluh, Peter. "Crack, the Contras, and the CIA: The Storm Over 'Dark Alliance.'" *Columbia Journalism Review*, Feb. 1997.

[5] "Digital Voice. Crack, The CIA and Media – All Complicit in Destroying Black Communities." *The Digital Voice*, 16 Dec. 2016, http://wordpress.philau.edu/thevoice/2016/12/crack-the-cia-and-media-all-complicit-in-destroying-Black-communities/

[6] Golden, Tim. "Though Evidence in Thin, Tale of CIA Drugs Has a Life of Its Own." *The New York Times*, 21 Oct. 1996.

[7] "Freeway: Crack in the System." *Al Jazeera America*, 2015.

[8] Taxy, Sam, Samuels, Julie, and William Adams. "Drug Offenders in Federal Prison: Estimates of Characteristics Based on Linked Data." Urban Institute U.S. Department of Justice: Bureau of Justice Statistics, Oct 2015, https://www.bjs.gov/content/pub/pdf/dofp12.pdf

[9] Whitehead, John. "Jailing Americans for Profit: The Rise of the Prison Industrial Complex." *HuffPost*, 10 June 2012, https://www.huffingtonpost.com/john-w-whitehead/prison-privatization_b_1414467.html

[10] Represent Us. "The Political Bribe that Turned Prisoners into Profits." https://represent.us/action/private-prisons-1/

[11] Williams, Timothy. "Privately Run Mississippi Prison, Called a Scene of Horror, Is Shut Down." *The New York Times*, 15 Sept 2016.

[12] "The President's Commission on Combating Drug Addiction and the Opioid Crisis." *The White House*, 1 Nov. 2017, https://www.whitehouse.gov/opioids/

[13] Assari, Shevin and Maryam Moghani Lankarani. "Association Between Stressful Life Events and Depression; Intersection of Race and Gender." *Journal of Racial and Ethnic Health Disparities*, June 2016, vol 3, no. 2, pp. 349-356.

[14] Modan, Naaz. "How America has Silently Accepted the Rage of White Men." *CNN*. 4 Oct 2017.

[15] Substance Abuse and Mental Health Services Administration. "Prescription Drug Misuse and Abuse." 30 Oct. 2017, https://www.samhsa.gov/topics/prescription-drug-misuse-abuse

[16] Sit, Ryan. "Trump Thinks Only Black people Are on Welfare, but, Really, White Americas Receive Most Benefits." *Newsweek.* 12 Jan. 2018.

[17] Dixon, Travis L. "A Dangerous Distortion of Our Families." *Color of Change,* Dec. 2017, https://colorofchange.org/dangerousdistortion/#report

[18] Jones, Jo and William Mosher. "Fathers' Involvement With Their Children: United States, 2006-2010." *National Health Statistic Reports,* 20 Dec. 2013, vol. 71.

[19] Taylor, Myiesha. "From Doc McStuffins to Black Panther: On-screen Diversity Drives Off-Screen STEM/STEAM Success." *State of Black America,* May, 2018, http://soba.iamempowered.com/doc-mcstuffins-Black-panther-screen-diversity-drives-screen-stemsteam-success

[20] Rose, Steve. "Repressed Brits, Evil Mexicans, Arab Villains: Why Are Hollywood's Animated Movies Full of Racist Stereotypes?" *The Guardian,* 6 April 2014.

[21] Madrigal, Alexis. "The Racist Housing Policy that Made Your Neighborhood." *The Atlantic,* 22 May 2014.

[22] Mitchell, Bruce. "HOLC 'Redlining' Maps: The Persistent Structure of Segregation and Economic Inequality." 20 Mar 2018.

[23] Jan, Tracy. "Redlining Was Banned 50 Years Ago. It's Still Hurting Minorities Today." *The Washington Post,* 28 March 2018.

[24] Chang, Alvin. "The Data Proves that School Segregation is Getting Worse." *Vox,* 5 Mar. 2018.

[25] Assari, Shervin, et al. "Subjective Socioeconomic Status Moderates the Association between Discrimination and Depression in African American Youth." *Brain Sciences,* vol 8, no. 4, 20 April 2018, http://www.mdpi.com/2076-3425/8/4/71/htm

[26] Gligon, John and Robert Gebeloff. "Affluent and Black, and Still Trapped by Segregation." *The New York Times,* 20 Aug. 2016, https://www.nytimes.com/2016/08/21/us/milwaukee-segregation-wealthy-Black-families.html

Jan, Tracy. "News Media Offers Consistently Warped Portrayals of Black Families, Study Finds." *The Washington Post,* 13 Dec. 2017.

Adelson, Bruce L. "Cartoon Villains, Diversity, and Implicit Bias." *Bromberg Translations,* 21 Feb. 2018. https://brombergtranslations.com/2018/02/21/cartoon-villains-diversity-and-implicit-bias/

Milman, Oliver. "Environmental Justice in America. A Civil Rights Emergency:

Justice, Clean Air and Water in the Age of Trump." *The Guardian*, 20 Nov. 2017, https://www.theguardian.com/us-news/2017/nov/20/environmental-justice-in-the-age-of-trump

Mikati, Ihab and Adam Benson. "Disparities in Distribution of Particulate Matter Emmi son Sources by Race and Poverty Status." *American Public Health Association*, Apr. 2018.

Bravo, Mercedes, et al. "Racial Isolation and Exposure to Airborne Particulate Matter and Ozone in Understudies US Populations: Environmental Justice Applications of Downscaled Numerical Model Output." *Environment International*, July-Aug. 2016, vol. 92-93, , pp. 247-255.

Drum, Kevin. "Lead: America's Real Criminal Element." *Mother Jones*, 11 Feb. 2016. https://www.motherjones.com/environment/2016/02/lead-exposure-gasoline-crime-increase-children-health/

Cabrera, Yvette. "Urban Children are Playing in Toxic Dirt." *Think Progress*, 12 July 2017.

Chang, Alvin. "White America is Quietly Self-Segregating." Vox, 18 Jan. 2017.

Vaidyanathan, Rajini. "Why Don't Black and White Americans Live Together?" *BBC News*. 8 Jan. 2016.

http://www.bbc.com/news/world-us-canada-35255835

Gladwell, Malcolm. *Outliers: The Story of Success*, Reprint Edition. Back Bay Books, 2011.

Bridge, Jeffrey and Lisa Horowitz. "Age-Related Racial Disparity in Suicide Rates Among U.S. Youth." *JAMA Pediatrics*, 21 May 2018

Gopnik, Adam. "The Caging of America. Why Do We Lock Up So Many People?" *The New Yorker*, 30 Jan. 2012.

## Being Black and Tested

[1] Thomas, P.L. "The Lingering, Powerful Legacy of 'Scientific Racism' in America." *Huffpost*, 9 Oct 2017, https://www.huffingtonpost.com/entry/the-lingering-and-powerful-legacy-of-scientific_us_59d0d76ee4b0f58902e5cd14


Steele, Claude M. "Thin Ice: Stereotype Threat and Black College Students." *The Atlantic Monthly*, Aug. 1999, vol. 284, no. 2, pp. 44-47, 50-54.

Steele, Claude M. and J. Aronson. "Stereotype threat and the intellectual test performance of African-Americans." *Journal of Personality and Social Psychology*, 1995, vol. 69, pp. 797-811.

"The Diaspora Prepared to Invest in Africa." *African Development Bank Group*, 30 May 2013, https://www.afdb.org/en/news-and-events/the-diaspora-prepared-to-invest-in-africa-11881/

Shahadah, Alik. "African Holocaust." 26 Jan. 2018, http://africanholocaust.net/africanholocaust/

"A Brief History of the SAT." *PBS Frontline*, https://www.pbs.org/wgbh/pages/frontline/shows/sats/where/history.html

Delmore, Erin. "SAT Scores Trend with Family Income." *MSNBC*, 7 Mar. 2014.

## Being Schooled

[1]   Palestini, Robert H. and Karen Palestini. Law and American Education: An Instructor's Guide. *The Scarecrow Press*, Inc, 2002.

"To Understand Schools We Must View Them in Historical Perspective." *Psychology Today*, 20 Aug. 2008, https://www.psychologytoday.com/us/blog/freedom-learn/200808/brief-history-education

Hamburger, Philip. *Separation of Church and State*. Harvard University Press. 2012.

McGreevy, John T. *Catholicism and American Freedom*. W.W. Norton. 2003.

Rosenthal, Robert and Jacobson, Lenore. *Pygmalion in the Classroom: Teacher Expectation and Pupils' Intellectual Development*. Holt, Rinehart & Winston, 1968.

Boser, Ulrich, Wilhelm, Megan, and Robert Hanna. "The Power of the Pygmalion Effect. Teachers Expectations Strongly Predict College Completion." *American Progress*, 6 Oct. 14, https://www.americanprogress.org/issues/education-k-12/reports/2014/10/06/96806/the-power-of-the-pygmalion-effect/

## Being Black and Schooled

[1]   Miron, Gary, Urschel, Jessica, Mathis, William, and Tornquist, Elana. "Schools without Diversity: Education Management Organizations, Charter Schools and the Demographic Stratification of the American School System." *Boulder and Tempe: Education and the Public Interest Center & Education Policy Research Unit*, 2011.

[2]   Gershenson, Hart, et al. "The Long-Run Impacts of Same-Race Teachers." *Institute of Labor Economics*, Mar. 2017.

[3] Dee, Thomas S. "The Race Connection." *Education Next*, Spring 2004, vol 4, no 2.

[4] Oakley, Deirdre, Stowell, Jacob, and John R. Logan. "The Impact of Desegregation on Black Teachers in the Metropolis, 1970-2000." *Ethnic Racial Study*, 2009, vol. 39, no. 9, pp. 1576-1598.

[5] Green, Ashley. "What is the Impact of the Exodus of Black Teachers?" *Texas A&M Today*, Oct. 2017, https://today.tamu.edu/2017/10/19/what-is-the-impact-of-the-exodus-of-Black-teachers/

[6] Kirwan Institute. "State of Science: Implicit Bias Review," 2015, http://kirwaninstitute.osu.edu/research/understanding-implicit-bias/

[7] Banaji, Mahzarin R. and Anthony G. Greenwald. *Blind Spot: Hidden Biases of Good People.* https://www.amazon.com/Blindspot-Hidden-Biases-Good-People/dp/1491528869

[8] Hoffman, Kelly M., et al. "Racial Bias in Pain Assessment and Treatment Recommendations, and False Beliefs about Biological Differences between Blacks and Whites." *Proceedings of the National Academy of Sciences of the United States of America*, April 2016, vol. 113, no. 16, pp. 4296-4301, http://www.pnas.org/content/113/16/4296

[9] Stanford Center on Poverty & Inequality. "State of the Union." 2017, https://inequality.stanford.edu/publications/pathway/state-union-2017

[10] Tajeu, Gabriel, et al. "Exploring the Association of Healthcare Worker Race and Occupation with Implicit and Explicit Racial Bias." *Journal of the National Medical Association*, 27 Dec 2017, https://doi.org/10.1016/j.jnma.2017.12.001

[11] Grant, Tobin. "Poll: Most Whites Say Blacks Are Lazier or Less Intelligent than Whites." *Religion News Service*, 8 Dec. 2014.

[12] Young, Yolanda. "Teaches' Implicit Bias against Black Students Starts in Preschool, Study Finds." *The Guardian*, 4 Oct. 2016, https://www.theguardian.com/world/2016/oct/04/Black-students-teachers-implicit-racial-bias-preschool-study

[13] Gershenson, Seth, Holt, Stephen, and Nicholas Papageorge. "Who believes in me? The effect of student–Teacher Demographic Match on Teacher Expectations." *Economics of Education Review*, June 2016, vol. 52, pp. 209-224.

[14] Van den Bergh, Linda and Eddie Denessen. "The Implicit Prejudiced Attitudes of Teachers: Relations to Teacher Expectation and the Ethnic Achievement Gap." *American Educational Research Journal*, June 2010, vol. 47, no. 2, pp. 497-527.

[15] Smith, Edward J. and Shaun R. Harper. "Center For The Study of Race & Equity in Education. Disproportionate Impact of K-12 School Suspension and

Expulsion on Black Student in Southern States." *University of Pennsylvania,* 2015, https://equity.gse.upenn.edu/SouthernStates

[16] Finley, Taryn. "HBCU Alumni Are Thriving More than Black Grads of Other Schools, Study Shows." *Black Voices,* 29 Oct. 2015, https://www.huffingtonpost.com/entry/hbcu-alumni-are-thriving-more-than-Black-grads-of-other-schools-study-shows_us_56310c1be4b0631799107aaa

[17] Kamenetz, Anya. "To Be Young, 'Gifted' and Black, It Helps to Have a Black Teacher." *NPR Ed,* 20 Jan. 2016, https://www.npr.org/sections/ed/2016/01/20/463190789/to-be-young-gifted-and-Black-it-helps-to-have-a-Black-teacher

[18] Evans, Gavin. "Black Brain, White Brain. Is Intelligence Skin Deep?" *Project Implicit, Harvard University,* 20 Jan. 2016, https://implicit.harvard.edu/implicit/takeatest.html


Grissom, Jason A. and Christopher Redding. "Discretion and Disproportionality: Explaining the Underrepresentation of High-Achieving Students of Color in Gifted Programs." *AERA Open,* 18 Jan 2016.

Anderson, Melinda. "The Radical Self-Reliance of Black Homeschooling." *The Atlantic,* 17 May 2018.

The Constitution of the United States of America.

U.S Government Accountability Office. "K-12 Education: Discipline Disparities for Black Students, Boys, and Students with Disabilities." 22 Mar. 2018, https://www.gao.gov/products/GAO-18-258

Civil Rights Data Collection (CRDC). https://ocrdata.ed.gov/

Texas Care for Children. "Keeping Kids in Class – Pre-K through 2nd Grade Suspensions in Texas and a Better Way Forward." Mar. 2018, http://txchildren.org/posts/2018/3/23/report-shows-texas-students-in-pre-k-through-2nd-grade-still-at-risk-of-getting-suspended

U.S. Department of Education Office for Civil Rights. "New Release for 2016. 2013-2014 Civil Rights Data Collection: A First Look." 28 Oct 2016, https://www2.ed.gov/about/offices/list/ocr/docs/2013-14-first-look.pdf

Artemis Medical Society and The Greenlining Institute. "Breaking Down Barriers for Women Physicians of Color," 25 Oct. 2017, http://greenlining.org/publications/2017/breaking-barriers-women-physicians-color/

Hutson, Matthew. "*Blindspot: Hidden Biases of Good People* by Mahzarin R. Banaji and Anthony G. Greenwald." *The Washington Post,* 8 Feb. 2013.

Turner, Cory. "Bias Isn't Just a Police Problem, It's A Preschool Problem." *NPR*

*Ed*, 28 Sept. 2016, https://www.npr.org/sections/ed/2016/09/28/495488716/bias-isnt-just-a-police-problem-its-a-preschool-problem

Miraya Ross, Kihana. "Let Our Black Children—and the Lofty Idea of School Integration—Go," 8 Dec. 2017, https://mlk50.com/let-our-Black-children-and-the-lofty-idea-of-school-integration-go-d304f41b0716


## Part 2

[1] Loewus, Liana. "The Nation's Teaching Force is Still Mostly White and Female." *Education Week*, 15 Aug. 2017

[2] Bush, Melodye. Ryan, Mommy, and Stephanie Rose. "Number of Instructional Days/Hours in the School Year." *Education Commission of the States*, Aug. 2011.

[3] National Center for Education Statistics. "Indicator 24: Time in Formal Instruction," 1991, https://nces.ed.gov/pubs/eiip/eiipid24.asp

[4] Murray, Linda. "Improving College Access and Success: Lessons Learned." *The Education Trust-West*, 12 Mar. 2000

[5] Lazarin, Melissa. "Testing Overload in America's Schools." *Center for American Progress*, 16 Oct. 2014.

[6] Mdzinarishvili, David. "America Hates Its Gifted Kids." *Newsweek*, 16 Jan. 2014.

[7] National Center for Education Statistics. "Program for International Student Assessment (PISA) 2012 Results." https://nces.ed.gov/surveys/pisa/pisa2012/index.asp

[8] Walker, Tim. "Classroom Shock: What I Am Learning as a Teacher in Finland." *Education Week Teacher*, 26 Nov. 2013.

[9] Assari, Shevin, and Maryam Moghani Lankarani. "Association Between Stressful Life Events and Depression; Intersection of Race and Gender." *Journal of Racial and Ethnic Health Disparities*, June 2016, vol. 3, no. 2, pp. 349-356.

[10] Woodson, Carter G. *The Mis-Education of the Negro*. Oshun Publishing. 1933.


Weller, Chris. "Homeschooling is the Smartest Way to Teach Kids in the 21st Century." *Business Insider*, 20 Aug. 2016.

Weber, Sam and Connie Kargbo Connie. "Black Families Increasingly Choose to Homeschool Kids." *PBS News Hour*, 22 April 2018.

Williams, Bonnie and Lawrence Williams. "The Socialization Myth." *Oak Meadow Independent Learning*, https://oakmeadow.com/resources/the-socialization-myth/

Okolosie, Lola. "Racism in Schools isn't Just Part of the Grim Past – It's Hiding in Plain Sight." *The Guardian*, 7 July 2017.

Page, Clarence. "Survivor Guilt: The Angst of the Black Bourgeoisie." *The Baltimore Sun*, 11 Mar. 1996.